PRAIRIE STATE COLLEGE LEARNING CENTER

00005 2889

P9-ECV-901

80578

Vietnam

by Harry Nickelson

LUCENT
B·O·O·K·S

LUCENT Overview Series

PRAIRIE STATE COLLEGE
LEARNING CENTER

Library of Congress Cataloging-in-Publication Data

Nickelson, Harry.
  Vietnam.

  (Lucent overview series)
  Includes bibliographical references.
  Summary: An account of the Vietnamese Conflict and
its aftermath, with information on its origins and
on how the war affected American foreign policy and
attitudes even today.
  1. Vietnamese Conflict, 1961-1975—Juvenile literature. 2. Vietnamese Conflict, 1961-1975—United States—
Juvenile literature. 3. United States—History—1945-
—Juvenile literature. [1. Vietnamese Conflict, 1961-
1975] I. Title. II. Series.
DS557.7.N53 1989   959.9   89-13100
ISBN 1-56006-110-3

No part of this book may be reproduced or used in any form or by any means, electrical,
mechanical, or otherwise, including, but not limited to, photocopy, recording, or any information storage and retrieval system, without prior written permission from the publisher.

© Copyright 1989 by Lucent Books, Inc.
P.O. Box 289011, San Diego, CA 92128-9011

Look for these and other books in the Lucent Overview series:

AIDS
Dealing with Death
Endangered Species
Garbage
Homeless Children
Smoking
Special Effects in the Movies
Vietnam

The editor wishes to thank Brad Steffens for his valuable contribution to this book.

Contents

Introduction

Every year, millions of tourists visit Washington, D.C. Most want to see the many monuments and buildings that preserve American history, places like the Washington Monument, the Lincoln and Jefferson Memorials, and the White House. Many people hope that by visiting these sites, they will feel closer to the men and women who helped make the United States what it is today. In recent years, however, the monument visited by more people than any other has not been one of those mentioned above. It is an angular wall of black granite located near the Washington Monument—the Vietnam Veterans Memorial.

Why do so many people visit this memorial? Why is it important to so many people?

Part of the answer may lie in its inscriptions. The names of 58,156 American soldiers who died or are missing in Vietnam have been etched into its polished surface. Many relatives of these men and women are still living. Thousands visit the memorial each year to see the names of those they loved and to remember them. Many visitors leave behind mementos, small gifts to the dead: notes, poems, a lock of hair, a graduation tassel. One mother left behind a baseball inscribed with the words, "To Carl, March 22, 1969, Love Mom." For those who lost loved ones in the war, the memory of Vietnam is personal and painful.

Others who visit the Vietnam Memorial are veterans who survived the war and their families and friends. For many veterans, the memorial is a symbol that the American people recognize the sacrifices they made for their country. Many veterans come to pay their respects to buddies they saw die in combat. Some veterans also leave behind mementos, often objects that relate to the war itself: combat boots, a North Vietnamese army shirt, an American M-14 rifle. Pete Martin of San Diego, California, left twelve Marine Corps battle ribbons at the base of the memorial. Martin laid his ribbons near the name of Louis Alonzo, a fellow soldier who was killed on a day when he had taken Martin's duty assignment. "Louie never got any of those ribbons," said Martin. "So I just thought I would give him mine."

A visitor to the Vietnam Veterans Memorial expresses anguish as painful memories possess him. Many visitors are deeply moved by the simple, black granite wall engraved with the names of the Vietnam War's casualties.

Other visitors are drawn to the Vietnam Memorial to remember not just the sacrifices made by those who fought in the war, but also the sacrifices made by those who tried to stop it. Millions of Americans protested the war in Vietnam. They walked in peace marches and occupied public buildings in sit-ins. On May 4, 1970, during an antiwar protest at Kent State University in Ohio, four youths were killed by members of the National Guard who were trying to restore order to the campus. Many others who resisted the war went to prison for their actions. Thousands of young men left the United States to avoid being drafted to serve in the war. To those who opposed the war, the Vietnam Memorial is a silent reminder of their cause as well.

Most people who visit the Vietnam Memorial did not suffer the loss of loved ones to the war or the protest movement, but they did suffer the war's pain. They were distressed when they saw film of the fighting in Vietnam, footage that was broadcast on the television news almost nightly. At work, in churches, at schools, and in homes, Americans argued about the war in Vietnam as they had no conflict since the Civil War. Across the country, small battles were fought over a large question: Should the United States be in Vietnam?

In 1975, the last American troops left Vietnam, and that question stopped being an issue. But confusion about the U.S. involvement in Vietnam has continued to haunt many Americans. Many people wonder why the U.S. got involved in Vietnam in the first place. They still question if it was right to send American troops to fight the war. They speculate about how the U.S. might have won the war, and they wonder why it did not.

It may be that, more than anything else, it is unanswered questions like these that draw so many to the Vietnam Memorial. Perhaps some of these questions can never be answered. But the 58,156 names carved into the memorial remind us that they are questions worth asking.

CHAPTER ONE

Why Did the United States Become Involved in Vietnam? (1950)

Vietnam is one of six countries on a peninsula known as Indochina. This peninsula juts out from the mainland of Asia deep into the South China Sea and the Indian Ocean. The other countries of Indochina are Burma, Thailand, Cambodia, Laos, and Malaysia.

Indochina received its name because the peninsula is located between India and China. Throughout history, these two large countries have influenced the smaller countries of Indochina. India's influence has been greatest in the western part of Indochina. China's influence has been greatest in the eastern part of Indochina, especially in Vietnam.

Vietnam lies along the eastern seaboard of the Indochinese peninsula. It is separated from the rest of Indochina by the Annamite Range, a chain of mountains that stretch southward from China and run parallel to the coast of Vietnam. These craggy mountains are covered with dense rain forests. In some places, these mountains stretch all the way across Vietnam to the coast. In other places, rivers have carved valleys and formed rich, flat deltas that are ideal for farming.

Few Americans had been to, or even heard of, Vietnam before June 27, 1950. This was the date on which President Harry Truman ordered the first American soldiers to go to Vietnam. The question is, why did he take this action?

President Truman sent troops to Vietnam to help France, which had been a close U.S. ally for many years. During the Revolutionary War, France was one of the first nations to recognize and support the United States, providing money and supplies that helped the Americans gain freedom from British colonial rule. More than a century later, France and the U.S. were still allies, fighting together in both World War I and World War II to defend Europe from domination.

Ironically, the support President Truman offered the French in 1950 was meant to help France continue its domination of a foreign country—its colonial rule of Vietnam. French forces had been in Vietnam since 1847, when they were first sent to protect French missionaries. Eventually, France colonized Vietnam, Cambodia, and Laos, a region that became known as French Indochina. The French gained goods and raw materials from Indochina. They also gained power by having military bases in Asia. The Vietnamese people resisted French rule, however, attacking French forces whenever they could.

Truman's mixed feelings

Although President Truman was eager to help France, he was not entirely pleased to be helping a colonial nation, especially one that was not popular with the native people. He demanded a "declaration by the French government of independence" for Vietnam and its neighbors, Laos and Cambodia. He said he would continue sending aid only if France promised to eventually allow the Vietnamese people to elect their own government.

Dwight Eisenhower, who succeeded Truman as president, agreed with this position. He said, "Among all the powerful nations of the world, the United States is the only one with a tradition of anti-colonialism." President Eisenhower let the French know that he expected them "to perfect the independence" of Vietnam.

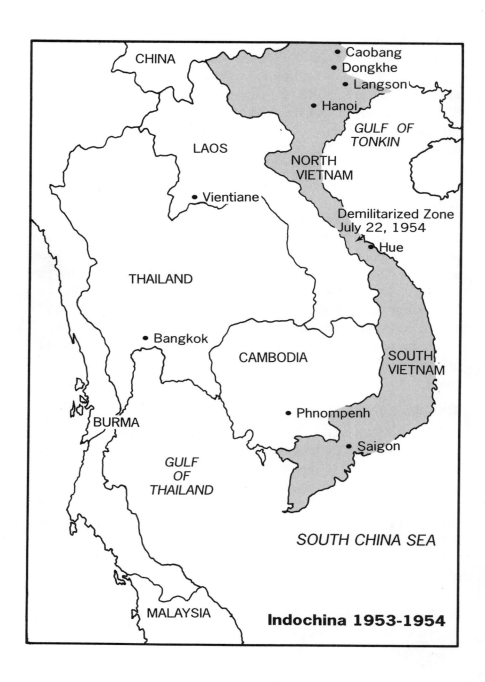

Indochina 1953-1954

Even though American leaders were not completely supportive of France's role in Vietnam, they disapproved of the forces that opposed France even more. From the U.S. point of view, French colonialism was the lesser of two evils. American leaders believed a greater evil was presented by France's opponent in Vietnam, a group known as the Vietminh.

The Vietminh was formed by a Vietnamese man named Ho Chi Minh. Like most Vietnamese, Ho Chi Minh did not want Vietnam to be ruled by a foreign power. He believed that Vietnam should be ruled by Vietnamese people. He knew that removing the French from power would be difficult, but he believed it could be done. He planned to use the principles of communism, which emphasize working together for the good of the whole group, to inspire and organize an uprising against the French. In 1929, he founded the Indochina Communist Party.

In 1940, French rule of Vietnam ended, but not in the way Ho Chi Minh had hoped. Japan, which had already occupied China, invaded Vietnam during World War II. Since France was occupied by the

North Vietnamese president Ho Chi Minh spent most of his life fighting for Vietnam's independence from various foreign rulers. He died in 1969 while his troops were still at war with American-aided South Vietnam.

Germans when Japan invaded, it was unable to defend its colony in Indochina. The Japanese soldiers quickly occupied Vietnam. The Japanese allowed the French to continue running the government, but the French had no real power. They had to do what the Japanese told them to do.

Ho Chi Minh was pleased to see the French weakened, but he did not want to see his country ruled by the Japanese either. In 1941, he formed a group to resist the Japanese occupation. He called the group the Viet Nam Doc Lap Dong Minh, which meant Vietnam Independence League. Soon the group came to be known simply as the Vietminh.

Defeating Japan takes precedence

The United States, which was also fighting against Japan, supported the Vietminh. American leaders distrusted Ho Chi Minh because he was a Communist, but during the war they cared more about defeating Japan than they did about Ho Chi Minh's beliefs. Just as the U.S. had joined forces with the Communist government of the Soviet Union to fight Nazi Germany in Europe, the U.S. joined with the Communist-led Vietminh to battle the Japanese. The U.S. supplied the Vietminh with weapons and helped train its fighters.

After Japan surrendered to the United States in August 1945, American leaders became concerned about the possibility of a Communist government assuming power in Vietnam. Within a few weeks, their worst fears were realized. With the French and the Japanese both weakened, Ho Chi Minh and other Vietnamese Communists formed the National Liberation Committee to take control of the Vietnamese government. On September 2, 1945, Ho Chi Minh declared the independence of the Democratic Republic of Vietnam. France did not recognize this new government, and neither did the United States. France opposed the Vietminh because it wanted to regain Vietnam as a colony. The United States opposed the Vietminh because it did not want to see a Communist government control Vietnam.

American leaders had opposed the idea of communism ever since it had been introduced by Karl Marx and Friedrich Engels in 1848. This is because the system of communism was seen to be the opposite of the system of capitalism practiced in the U.S. Communism limits the private ownership of property, allowing more people to share in a nation's wealth. Capitalism depends on the unlimited ownership of private property to inspire people to work harder and create more wealth. The two systems cannot exist in the same place at the same time. When Communists gain control of a capitalist country, individuals and businesses lose their property.

Marx also taught that the Communist system would work best if all people in all countries were united under its principles. His beliefs, known as Marxism, suggested that every nation that was able to form a Communist government had a duty to help other nations become Communist. This aspect of communism also disturbed leaders of capitalist countries like the U.S. They concluded that all Communists in all countries would work together to end capitalism worldwide.

Communism begins to spread

At first, communism did not pose a great threat to the U.S. Before World War II, only one country in the world, the Soviet Union, had a Communist government. After World War II, however, things changed. The Soviet army remained in the portions of eastern Europe it had occupied while defeating Nazi Germany. Following the principles of Marxism, the Soviet leaders used this military presence to install new Communist governments in several countries, including Czechoslovakia, Hungary, Poland, and the eastern half of Germany.

In 1949, American fears about the spread of communism increased. In China, Communist forces, supported by the Soviet Union, completed their conquest of the Chinese mainland. This event stunned the United States. It meant that Communist forces controlled the most populous nation in the world. It also meant that Communists con-

Harry S. Truman was U.S. president from 1945 to 1953. His policy of containing the spread of communism led to U.S. involvement in Korea and Vietnam.

trolled an unbroken mass of territory that stretched from central Europe, across Asia, to the Pacific Ocean.

John Foster Dulles, secretary of state from 1953 to 1959, argued that the Soviet Union, China, and the Communist countries of eastern Europe made up a solid bloc of cooperating nations. Speaking about Vietnam to the Overseas Press Club in 1953, Dulles said:

> Those fighting under the banner of Ho Chi Minh have largely been trained and equipped in Communist China. They are supplied with artillery and ammunition through the Soviet-Chinese Communist bloc. Captured material shows that much of it was fabricated by the Skoda Munition Works in Czechoslovakia and transported across Russia and Siberia and then sent through China into Vietnam.

By tracing the route by which these weapons were shipped to Vietnam, Dulles meant to show two things. First, he wanted to show that many Communist countries were working closely together to help Ho Chi Minh try to gain control of Vietnam. Second, he wanted to describe how weapons could be transported halfway around the world without ever leaving Communist soil.

Dwight D. Eisenhower was U.S. president from 1953 to 1961. His administration continued U.S. support to anti-Communist forces in Vietnam.

Dulles and other American officials began to use the term domino theory to describe the Communist threat in Asia. They believed that if the Communists were able to gain control of the government in Vietnam, they then would work to topple the governments in the neighboring countries of Laos and Cambodia. As these nations fell under Communist control, they would in turn topple the governments in the countries that shared their borders. In this manner, one nation after another would fall under Communist control, like a row of dominoes.

Critics of the domino theory

Not everyone in the U.S. believed in the domino theory or agreed that Communist forces were trying to dominate the world. Some observers pointed out that the Soviet Union had suffered greater losses than any other country during World War II. It seemed reasonable to them that the Soviet Union would want to retain control of bordering countries as a buffer against future attacks. They also argued that Communist revolutions occurred in countries like China and Vietnam not because of a worldwide plot by the Soviet Union, but because people in a poor country try to find new ways of distributing their nation's wealth.

Other Americans did not doubt that the Soviet leaders were trying to spread communism to other countries, but they felt it was not in the best interest of the U.S. to get involved in foreign conflicts. These people were known as isolationists because they believed the U.S. could and should remain as isolated from other nations as possible. They took very seriously George Washington's warning that the U.S. should avoid entangling alliances with foreign powers. The isolationists saw Soviet influence at work in eastern Europe and Asia, but they did not think there was anything the U.S. could or should do about it.

However, an event occurred on June 25, 1950, that caused many Americans, including some isolationists, to become seriously concerned about the spread of communism. On that date, forces from Communist North Korea invaded South Korea. Within four days, the Communists occupied the South Korean capital of Seoul. President Truman responded harshly to the Communist aggression. "The attack upon Korea makes it plain beyond all doubt that Communism . . . will now use armed invasion and war [to] conquer independent nations," Truman said. He immediately ordered American troops into Korea to repel the invasion.

Containment

The United Nations (UN), which had been established in 1948, supported Truman's decision to help South Korea defend itself against the invaders from the north. The UN Security Council passed a resolution calling on all members of the UN to give assistance to South Korea. Forty-two nations, including Australia, Great Britain, and the Philippines, joined forces with the United States to fight the North Korean army and the Chinese troops that supported it. Eventually, North Korean forces were driven back to the original border.

Truman's policy of containing, or holding back, the spread of communism appeared to have succeeded.

In December 1950, the U.S. formally extended the policy of containment throughout Southeast Asia, including Vietnam. On December 23, the U.S. signed the Mutual Defense Assistance Agreement with France, Vietnam, Cambodia, and Laos. In the words of Dean Rusk, who, in the 1950s, was the assistant secretary of state for Far Eastern affairs, the purpose of the assistance was to "preserve Indochina and Southeast Asia from further Communist encroachment."

Meanwhile, the governments of both the Soviet Union and China had recognized Ho Chi Minh's Communist government, the Democratic Republic of Vietnam, as the legal government of Vietnam. As the U.S. increased its aid to the French-backed regime that ruled the southern part of Vietnam, the Soviet Union and China increased their support of the Vietminh, which ruled the north. As 1950 drew to a close, the stage was set for an all-out war between the French and the Vietminh.

CHAPTER TWO

Why Did the French Leave Vietnam? (1950-1956)

By 1950, the French had regained control of the major cities of Vietnam: Saigon, in the south, and Haiphong and Hanoi, in the north. They did not, however, control the countryside. There, the Vietminh were able to fight the French to a standstill. They did it by using the dense jungle and mountainous terrain to their advantage. They hid in the foliage, then attacked the French troops from close range. This allowed the Vietminh to use a minimum number of bullets to kill a maximum number of French soldiers. The French were unable to fight back effectively because they were unable to see the enemy. The French army had been stopped by a technique of warfare the Vietnamese had developed nearly a thousand years earlier to fight the Chinese.

Development of guerrilla warfare

In 208 B.C., the Chinese invaded Vietnam. They ruled Vietnam for over a thousand years. In some ways, the Vietnamese benefited from the Chinese occupation. The Vietnamese adopted the Chinese alphabet and political system. They also began to practice the Buddhist religion, which teaches that peace of mind is reached through patience, selflessness, and meditation.

The Vietnamese also used the Chinese method of wet rice farming. This system requires many people to work together to plant and harvest the crops. Working together closely strengthened the loyalties among the Vietnamese people.

Eventually, the Vietnamese resented Chinese domination, and they began to fight for their freedom. In some ways, the practices they had learned from the Chinese helped the Vietnamese win their battle for independence. The loyalty and cooperation learned from collective farming helped them to unite in their struggle against the Chinese. The patience and selflessness taught by their religion helped them endure their long quest for independence.

Because the Chinese forces had better weapons, the Vietnamese had to fight a war of stealth and surprise. They attacked the Chinese on narrow mountain passes or in the dense jungle, then disappeared before the Chinese could respond with their superior power. The method of fighting later became known as guerrilla warfare.

Guerrilla attackers destroyed Chinese supply lines and killed many Chinese soldiers. This made the occupation of Vietnam costly for China. In 1428, the Chinese left Vietnam. Guerrilla warfare had provided a way for the Vietnamese to rid their country of the Chinese. Five hundred years later, the Vietminh used this same method against the French.

Guerrilla warfare and the French

Because guerrilla warriors often use simple weapons, those who fight the guerrillas sometimes underestimate their strength. In Vietnam, General Jacques Philippe Leclerc, the general in charge of returning the country to French control, greatly misjudged the effectiveness of the Vietminh guerrilla forces.

A distinguished leader in World War II, Leclerc predicted in 1946 that his army would defeat the Vietminh in four weeks. Four years later, the French army controlled even less territory than it had in 1946. In the cities, the French were able to locate Vietminh strongholds. The French then used their superior weapons to destroy the enemy positions. But in the countryside, the guerrillas disappeared into the jungle like bats into the night. The superior French weapons were useless against an enemy the French soldiers could not see.

Pacification

The only way for the French to conquer the unseen enemy was to cut the guerrillas off from the supplies they needed. Since they are not part of a regular army, guerrillas depend on civilians for food, clothing, shelter, and other necessities. Guerrilla warfare can be effective only if the guerrillas enjoy the widespread support of the common people. To defeat the Vietminh, the French needed to convince the Vietnamese people not to assist the guerrillas. This involved doing two things. First, they had to show the villagers who supported the Vietminh that they would be punished for their actions. Second, they had to show those who supported the French that they would be protected against Vietminh attacks. In short, the French had to demonstrate that they were in control of each village.

The commander of the French forces in Vietnam, General Jacques Philippe Leclerc, boasted that the French would defeat the Vietminh within four weeks.

Once a village was under control, it was considered peaceful, or pacified. When the French swept into a village, the guerrilla forces usually retreated into the jungle and waited for the French to leave. The French pacification remained effective only as long as French soldiers stayed in the village to show that they were in control. As soon as the French soldiers left a village, the Vietminh returned. The guerrillas obtained supplies from those who supported them, and they murdered those who had cooperated with the French. As the French historian Philippe Devillers put it, "If we departed, believing a region pacified, the Vietminh would arrive at our heels."

The French did not have enough troops to occupy every village in Vietnam, so they built a system of fortresses. These military outposts were designed to keep an area pacified by keeping the guerrillas away from the villages. The most important of these fortresses were placed in the Red River Delta, between Hanoi and Haiphong in the north.

The Red River Delta is the most populous area of northern Vietnam. It is also the center of northern Vietnam's farming and industry. The French knew they had to control the Red River Delta if they were to realize their dream of once again ruling Vietnam. Ho Chi Minh understood the importance of the Red River Delta, too. When he was driven out of Hanoi by the French, he retreated to an area known as the Viet Bac. From this area, his Vietminh forces could enter and attack the Red River Delta.

The Vietminh surprise the French

With the same guerrilla warfare methods their ancestors had used against the Chinese, the Vietminh began to disrupt French supply lines to the fortresses in the Red River Delta. They ambushed French convoys, killing soldiers and destroying supplies, then quickly retreated into the underbrush. The surprised French forces tried to strike back, but rarely could they locate the Vietminh guerrillas.

French attempts to keep the Vietminh out of the villages also met

A French artillery unit shells Vietminh-held villages north of Hanoi in what later became North Vietnam. Despite such firepower, the French could not stop the determined Vietminh.

resistance. The Vietminh simply hid while the French soldiers patrolled the jungle during the day. When the French troops returned to their fortresses after sunset, the Vietminh reentered the villages. Under the cover of darkness, the Vietminh obtained food and supplies from the villagers. They also held meetings, encouraging the villagers not to cooperate with the French. When they found out that villagers had helped the French, the Vietminh executed them. Using these methods, the Vietminh controlled 1,486 of 2,700 villages in the Red River Delta in mid-1953.

By 1953, the French had grown discouraged with the progress of the war. The Vietminh had surrounded many of their outposts, so supplies to these fortresses had to be dropped by parachute. The Vietminh had also moved into the neighboring country of Laos to avoid the French patrols and to obtain food and supplies from the Laotian villagers. This increased the size of the area the French had to try to pacify. Because their forces were being stretched too thinly across the countryside, the French decided they had to change their strategy. Instead of trying to defend every village against the Vietminh, they had to find the guerrilla hideouts and attack them.

In November 1953, French paratroopers drove the Vietminh from the village of Dien Bien Phu. This village was in a valley west of the Viet Bac, just ten miles from the Laotian border. The French hoped to use this remote outpost to attack the Vietminh hiding in the jungle of the Viet Bac. They also hoped to use this outpost to stop further movements of the Vietminh soldiers into Laos.

The French quickly went to work turning the village into a fortress. They tore the buildings apart to make bunkers and command posts. They cleared and leveled land to create an airstrip so they could

A French paratrooper, his parachute still lying beneath him, fires an automatic rifle in the French attack on Dien Bien Phu, November 20, 1953. The attack was successful, but the Vietminh recaptured the city six months later.

receive supplies. More and more troops arrived, until fifteen thousand French soldiers occupied the valley.

The French felt reasonably safe in Dien Bien Phu. They were convinced the site was too remote for the Vietminh to mass their troops and weapons for a major attack. They were wrong.

Led by the brilliant general, Vo Nguyen Giap, the Vietminh began moving large numbers of troops and huge amounts of supplies to the hills surrounding Dien Bien Phu. Many Vietnamese civilians resented French rule, so they helped the Vietminh. They cut new paths through the jungles so they could transport weapons and supplies without the French spotting them from the air and bombing them. The civilians did much of their work at night, using specially made bicycles called iron horses to carry weapons, bullets, and food to Dien Bien Phu. Meanwhile, forty thousand Vietminh soldiers, marching twenty miles a night, poured into the hills around Dien Bien Phu from as far as five hundred miles away.

Hauling artillery across the jungle

Most surprisingly, the Vietminh hauled the world's largest artillery and antiaircraft guns across the Vietnamese terrain to Dien Bien Phu. The Vietminh and their supporters pulled these cannons, which were mounted on wheels, by hand through the Vietnamese mountains and jungle. The Vietnminh placed these cannons in the openings of caves around the rim of the valley. These weapons were so well hidden that the French could not locate them even when the Vietminh began firing on them on the afternoon of March 12, 1954.

Within hours, the cannons destroyed the airfield the French had built. The Vietminh overran several outlying command posts, killing five hundred French soldiers. The French still held their main fortress, but they were cut off from all supplies except those dropped by parachute.

Instead of launching an attack on the main fortress, the Vietminh began digging trenches and tunnels in the valley floor. By late April,

Vietnamese soldiers receive training in 1962 from U.S. Army adviser Major Elmer J. Gainok (second from right).

they had dug within a few hundred yards of the French stronghold. At night, as French soldiers ate their rations, they could hear the scraping of Vietminh shovels as the enemy dug nearer and nearer, preparing for the final assault. Still, the Vietminh did not attack. They were waiting for the moment when world leaders thousands of miles away, in Geneva, Switzerland, would begin to discuss their country's struggle.

The Geneva Accords

Leaders from the United States, Great Britain, the Soviet Union, and China had gathered in Geneva to see if they could find a way to settle both the Korean War and the fighting in Vietnam. On May 7, 1954, just as the members of the conference were about to discuss

Vietnam, the Vietminh attacked. As the entire world looked on, the Vietminh captured Dien Bien Phu within hours.

The Vietminh had lost close to eight thousand soldiers in the battle over Dien Bien Phu. The French had lost more than three thousand. Another eight thousand French soldiers were taken prisoner by the Vietminh and were forced to march five hundred miles to be imprisoned in the Red River Delta. More than half of these captives died during the march or in prison.

Ho Chi Minh in control

The battle at Dien Bien Phu convinced the leaders in Geneva that Ho Chi Minh's forces were definitely in control of northern Vietnam. The participants in the conference decided the simplest thing to do was to divide Vietnam into two parts at the seventeenth parallel. Parallels are the horizontal lines on maps and globes. The seventeenth parallel runs through the middle of Vietnam. The area north of this line was to be ruled by Ho Chi Minh's government. The area south of this line was to be ruled not by the French, but by an independent, non-Communist state. This nation, known as the Republic of South Vietnam, was to be led by Ngo Dinh Diem.

The leaders in Geneva did not mean to divide Vietnam permanently. The Geneva Accords, as this agreement came to be known, stated that elections were to be held in Vietnam in 1956. At this time, the people of Vietnam would elect one government to rule the entire country. This government would reunite the two Vietnams into one independent nation.

The U.S. and the government of South Vietnam did not sign the Geneva Accords. Leaders of both countries were afraid these elections would mean that Ho Chi Minh's Communist government would rule all Vietnam. American leaders feared that their policy of containment would fail.

After the Geneva Accords, French forces left Vietnam for the last time, 107 years after their arrival.

CHAPTER THREE

Why Did the United States Send Troops to Vietnam? (1956-1964)

Ngo Dinh Diem did not hold the nationwide elections in 1956 that were called for by the Geneva Accords. He feared that the Communists might try to force people to vote for them, or worse, that Ho Chi Minh might win the election outright. Diem's failure to hold elections disturbed many people in South Vietnam who were critical of Diem. It also caused unrest among those who supported Ho Chi Minh and wanted to see Vietnam unified under his leadership.

The supporters of Ho Chi Minh in South Vietnam became known as the Vietcong, which means Communist Vietnamese. After Diem refused to hold elections, the Vietcong began fighting the forces of Diem's government, again using the techniques of guerrilla warfare. The Vietcong were supported in their efforts by Ho Chi Minh's government in North Vietnam. They also received support from the Soviet Union and China.

The U.S. continued to support Diem, even after he refused to hold elections. President Eisenhower promised U.S. aid to Diem in a letter:

> We have been exploring ways and means to permit our aid to Vietnam to be more effective and to make a greater contribution to the welfare and stability of the Government of Vietnam . . .

> The Government of the United States expects that this aid will
> be met by performance on the part of the Government of Viet-
> nam in undertaking needed reforms.

As the letter makes clear, President Eisenhower supported Diem's government. But the American president also believed that great reforms were needed. Eisenhower expected Diem to hold free elections and give the Vietnamese people greater freedom.

The Diem dilemma

As the Eisenhower letter suggests, the U.S. had mixed feelings about Diem. He was a strong anti-Communist, which pleased American leaders. But Diem ruled his country in a way that distressed many American officials. He limited the freedom of the press, placed his critics in prison without trials, and restricted the practice of religion. As before, with the French, the U.S. found itself supporting the lesser of two evils in Vietnam.

Many Vietnamese people also disapproved of Diem's policies, especially the restrictions he placed on religious freedom. Diem was a Christian, which made him part of a religious minority in Vietnam. As president, he feared the power of the Buddhists, the largest religious group in Vietnam. Because of these fears, Diem followed the French tradition of requiring Buddhists to obtain permission from the government before holding public events.

Diem was also unpopular with Vietnamese villagers because of the methods his forces used to fight the Vietcong. Like the French, Diem's forces realized that the guerrillas depended on the support of the people to fight effectively. To keep villagers from helping the Vietcong, Diem's troops devised what was known as the strategic hamlet program. The plan was to move the Vietnamese out of their villages and into hamlets that were fortified against the Vietcong. This kept the villagers and the Vietcong apart, making it harder for the guerrillas to obtain necessary food and supplies.

Strategic hamlets were surrounded by moats filled with sharpened bamboo sticks. The only way into the hamlets was through a guarded gate. Although designed to keep the Vietcong out of hamlets, the fortifications also kept the villagers in. Many villagers resented this, especially those who had been forced to leave their homes to live in the hamlets.

Not only were strategic hamlets unpopular, they were also ineffective. The Vietcong often found ways into the strategic hamlets. Either they were helped by villagers who supported them, or they dug tunnels under the moats. Once inside, the Vietcong not only got food and supplies, they also stirred up the villagers against Diem.

The fall of Diem

The growing unpopularity of Diem disturbed American leaders, including President John F. Kennedy, who had been elected in 1960. Kennedy saw Vietnam as "a proving ground for democracy in Asia . . . the alternative to a Communist dictatorship." He feared that

South Vietnamese president Ngo Dinh Diem waves as his motorcade moves through downtown New York in 1957. American leaders had severe doubts about Diem's ability to lead his country but continued their support.

*John F. Kennedy,
U.S. president from
1961 to 1963,
worried that Diem's
unpopularity with
his people would
ruin the chances for
democracy in
Vietnam.*

a government that did not have the sympathy and support of the people would be unable to defeat the Communist forces. Kennedy worried that Diem's unpopularity would spoil the chances for democracy to succeed in Vietnam.

In 1961, Kennedy sent a message to Frederick E. Nolting Jr., the U.S. ambassador to South Vietnam, telling him to let Diem know that continued U.S. support depended on Diem's ability to increase his popular support. At the very least, Kennedy wanted Diem to treat his critics less harshly and allow his people to have greater religious freedom. But Diem did not respond. Later, he would take steps in the opposite direction.

Buddhist protests

On May 1, 1963, Buddhists in the city of Hue gathered in the streets to protest a decree against flying their flag. Diem's troops broke up the demonstration by shooting into the crowd. Eight children and one woman were killed by the gunfire and the stampede the shooting had caused.

In the following months, thousands of Buddhists protested against Diem's oppression. On June 11, 1963, a Buddhist monk named Quang Duc sat down at a busy intersection in Saigon, surrounded by other monks and nuns. A fellow Buddhist poured gasoline over him. Another lit him on fire. Other Buddhists handed out a leaflet that included Quang Duc's plea that Diem extend charity and compassion to all religions. This grisly protest, captured on film by Associated Press photographer Malcolm Brown, shocked people in Vietnam and around the world. Diem himself was unmoved by Quang Duc's protest. In the following months, more monks set themselves on fire. These protests caused even more resentment of Diem in Vietnam.

On August 21, Diem's brother, Ngo Dinh Nhu, directed attacks against a number of Buddhist temples across Vietnam. Government forces broke into the major temple in Saigon and arrested four hundred monks and nuns. In Hue, Buddhist monks and nuns battled Nhu's forces for eight hours. These attacks sparked riots and demonstrations in Vietnam. They also caused the U.S. government to lose confidence in Diem's ability to lead his nation.

A Vietnamese Buddhist monk named Quang Duc allowed himself to be burned alive as a protest against the religious intolerance of the Diem regime. His dramatic plea to the government went unheeded.

President Kennedy instructed Henry Cabot Lodge, the new U.S. ambassador to Vietnam, to tell Diem that he had to remove his brother from power. If Diem did not cooperate, the U.S. would no longer support him. When Lodge spoke with Diem, the Vietnamese leader refused to go along with the plan. After this meeting, Ambassador Lodge informed the president that "there is no possibility, in my view, that the war can be won under a Diem administration."

A coup d'état

During his presidency, Diem had survived several attempts to remove him from power. During the Buddhist uprising, generals in Diem's army again began to plot the president's overthrow. After Diem refused to take action against his brother, Ambassador Lodge let the generals know that the U.S. would not attempt to interfere with a coup d'état (violent overthrow) of Diem's government. President Kennedy approved this language, but told Lodge to "avoid being drawn into reviewing or advising on operational plans, or any other act that might identify the United States too closely" with the coup. Kennedy and others feared that the generals might not succeed. Kennedy did not want the U.S. to be linked to a failed coup attempt.

On November 1, 1963, the coup d'état against the Diem government began. Rebel troops surrounded Diem's presidential palace. Soldiers loyal to Diem fought for hours to defend their president. Diem himself escaped during the fighting, slipping away to a hideout that his brother had prepared for just such an emergency. Diem negotiated with the new leaders, but they would not allow him to be part of the new government or even to resign publicly. They did promise him and his brother safe passage out of the country, however. Diem and Nhu were picked up by an armored car to be taken to the headquarters of the new leaders. They never made it. The car stopped at a railroad crossing, and the brothers were executed.

The Kennedy administration hoped that the new leaders in South Vietnam would gain the popular support required to defeat the Vietcong. Some members of the administration, however, doubted if this would be the case. Robert Kennedy, President Kennedy's brother and U.S. attorney general, wondered if the Vietcong could be resisted with any government in South Vietnam.

Other members of the administration believed the war against the Vietcong should continue. Dean Rusk, Kennedy's secretary of state, argued that the U.S. should not "pull out . . . until the war is won." Lyndon Johnson, vice president under Kennedy, believed the U.S. "should stop playing cops and robbers and go about winning the war." Johnson's attitude was important because three weeks after Diem was removed from power, John Kennedy was assassinated and Johnson became president.

When Johnson took office, he found that the situation in Vietnam had not improved as he and others in the Kennedy administration had hoped. When Diem was killed, North Vietnam began sending troops across the seventeenth parallel, into South Vietnam. The Vietcong also increased their attacks after Diem's death. The new government in South Vietnam needed more help from the U.S.

A squad leader of the U.S. 1st Air Cavalry Division calls for his troops to attack a Vietnamese hamlet.

Shortly after he became president, Johnson met with Ambassador Lodge about the situation in Vietnam. Johnson assured Lodge that he would not lose Vietnam to the Communists. He told the ambassador to ''tell those generals in Saigon that Lyndon Johnson intends to stand by our word.''

Johnson began shipping more supplies to South Vietnam. He also increased naval operations along the Vietnamese coast. On August 2, 1964, the U.S. warship *Maddox* was attacked by North Vietnamese gunboats in the Gulf of Tonkin, off the coast of North Vietnam.

The Gulf of Tonkin Resolution

In response to these attacks, President Johnson decided he had to take a strong stand against the North Vietnamese. He asked the U.S. Congress for the authority to ''take all necessary measures to repel any armed attack against the armed forces of the United States and to prevent further aggression.'' The U.S. House of Representatives unanimously approved Johnson's request, known as the Gulf of Tonkin Resolution. In the U.S. Senate, only two of fifty senators voted against the resolution. Wayne Morse of Oregon predicted the U.S. would live to regret the action. Ernest Gruening of Alaska said, ''All Vietnam is not worth the life of a single American boy.''

In November 1964, Johnson was reelected president. With the support of Congress, Johnson increased U.S. involvement in Vietnam. By the end of 1964, 23,500 American combat troops were stationed on Vietnamese soil. And more were on the way.

CHAPTER FOUR

Why Did the United States Stay in Vietnam? (1964-1968)

As American military involvement in Vietnam grew, American policy toward Vietnam changed. The general political goal of containing communism slowly became a specific military objective: to stop the Vietcong from spreading their influence. Decisions made in Washington by President Johnson were carried out in Vietnam by generals, colonels, captains, sergeants, and finally common foot soldiers, the "grunts," who slogged their way through the Vietnamese rice paddies.

U.S. troops began helping the South Vietnamese army plan and coordinate raids against the Vietcong. These military actions had military consequences. The Vietcong reacted to the American actions by attacking U.S. troops directly.

Escalation

When two sides in a conflict respond to each other's actions with greater and greater force, the process is known as escalation. Like the steps of an escalator, the number of soldiers rises higher and higher, and the number of battles, injuries, and deaths goes up with it. This is what happened in Vietnam. The Vietcong and the United

States began to fight each other with more and more soldiers and firepower.

When the number of attacks on U.S. servicemen increased in 1964, President Johnson decided to begin bombing North Vietnam, which helped the Vietcong with weapons and supplies. The bombing, in turn, led the Vietcong to attack more American troops. The U.S. responded by sending more troops to Vietnam. From December 1964 to June 1965, the number of American ground forces in Vietnam more than tripled, from 23,500 to 75,000.

Search and destroy missions

Before 1965, American soldiers had not been directly involved in the fighting against Vietcong guerrillas. The Americans had only supported and supplied the South Vietnamese soldiers, who were doing all the fighting. But in the summer of 1965, American soldiers staged their first combat mission, searching for villages controlled by the Vietcong, referred to as the VC, or Victor Charlies, by the Americans. The Americans fought the guerrillas and destroyed their supplies. These attacks, known as search-and-destroy missions, became the hallmark of U.S. military strategy in Vietnam.

When President Johnson sent American forces into combat, he took a giant step in the escalation of the war. Combat troops need protection and support. For every soldier who actually fights the enemy, many more soldiers are needed to provide communications, food, ammunition, and medical help. The air force and navy often assist ground troops with additional firepower. After the first American combat missions, General William Westmoreland, the military commander in charge of the U.S. troops in Vietnam, asked President Johnson to more than double the number of American troops already in Vietnam, to a total of 180,000.

On July 28, 1965, Johnson addressed the nation on television. He told the American people, ''I have asked the commanding general, General Westmoreland, what more he needs to meet this mounting

Lyndon B. Johnson, U.S. president from 1963 to 1969, greatly escalated American involvement in the Vietnam War. Johnson did not believe that the U.S. could be defeated by the Communists.

aggression. He has told me. And we will meet his needs. We cannot be defeated by force of arms. We will stand in Vietnam.''

General Westmoreland realized that American armed forces had never fought a war in jungles like those in Vietnam. He also knew that American forces had never faced an enemy like the Vietcong, a rugged, dedicated corps of guerrilla warriors. He believed a war against the Vietcong guerrillas would be won by reducing the numbers of the enemy. He called this strategy a war of attrition.

Westmoreland's methods

Westmoreland's approach differed from the strategy of conventional warfare. In conventional warfare fought by generals throughout history, from Alexander the Great and Julius Caesar to George Washington and General Eisenhower, military success is achieved by taking control of land. The goal is to push enemy forces out of cities, across plains, and over mountains along organized battlefronts. Soldiers' deaths, or casualties, are the result of battles for territory.

A war of attrition, however, is won not by capturing land. It is won by killing enemy troops. Success is measured not by the location of a battlefront, but by the number of enemy that have been killed.

American soldiers fought the war of attrition well. They killed several times more Vietcong troops than they lost themselves. But enemy deaths did not mean U.S. success. The problem was one of simple arithmetic. Ho Chi Minh had millions of guerrillas and North Vietnamese soldiers at his command. American troops numbered in the thousands. In the 1940s, Ho Chi Minh had told the French, "You can kill ten of my men for every one I kill of yours, but even at those odds, you will lose and I will win." His warning was still true in the 1960s.

To counter these odds, Westmoreland asked President Johnson to send even more troops to Vietnam. Johnson agreed. By the end of 1966, the number of U.S. forces reached four hundred thousand. It

U.S. Army medics rush a wounded soldier to an evacuation helicopter during a fierce battle for a strategically located piece of land near the Laotian border. The site became known as Hamburger Hill.

soon became clear that Westmoreland's war of attrition would not succeed quickly. It would require many more troops and several years of hard fighting.

The war of attrition posed unexpected problems for the American military and public. One problem was soldier morale. In a conventional war, combat troops can measure their success by the movement of the battlefront across the land. As soldiers conquer more territory, they gain more confidence and fight better. But the war of attrition did not have a battlefront. U.S. forces conquered and reconquered the same villages many times. The body counts, as the military called the numbers of casualties, showed many enemy deaths. But the soldiers and the American public could not see any real progress in the war effort. The lack of progress hurt soldier morale. Low morale made soldiers less effective, and this prolonged the war.

The war of attrition's morality debated

Another problem with the war of attrition was one of morality. Some people, particularly members of religious groups like the Society of Friends (Quakers) and Mennonites (Amish), believe war is immoral because it involves the taking of human life. Most Americans, however, believe war is sometimes justified. These people often describe war as a necessary evil. The evil of killing is balanced out by the necessity of defending people and land. Killing is viewed as an undesirable means to achieve a desirable end.

Even those who believed in justifiable wars had a hard time accepting Westmoreland's war of attrition. The strategy in Vietnam emphasized the evil of war—the killing—rather than the necessity of war—the securing of land. American troops appeared to be killing the enemy not as a means to achieve an end, but as an end in itself. This apparent killing for the sake of killing disturbed many Americans.

Americans were also troubled by the effect the war had on Vietnamese civilians. Nearly every war causes civilian deaths, but the

Vietnam War produced an unusually large number of civilian casualties. This is because the young American soldiers (their average age was nineteen) had a hard time identifying the enemy. Vietcong guerrillas did not wear uniforms. They hid among civilians in villages. Often the guerrillas were helped by women and children who planted bombs or threw hand grenades at the Americans. American soldiers were attacked while they were on patrol, while they slept, and even while they ate in restaurants. U.S. troops were surrounded by an enemy they could not identify, but one that could strike at any time. When U.S. forces moved into villages controlled by the Vietcong, civilians were often caught in the cross fire. Sometimes civilians were misidentified as the enemy and killed outright. The difficulty of identifying the enemy caused more civilian deaths and slowed the progress of the war.

Civilian casualties

The weapons the U.S. used in Vietnam added to the number of civilian casualties. Long-range weapons, like heavy artillery and guided missiles, easily strayed off target, exploding in civilian areas. President Johnson's campaign of continuous bombing of North Vietnam, known as Rolling Thunder, also caused a large number of civilian casualties. A new kind of bomb, the napalm bomb, also had dire effects on civilians. These bombs contained a sticky goo that ignited as quickly as gasoline does. Napalm bombs were used in areas where the Vietcong could not be removed by American troops. If the napalm accidentally splashed on a civilian, the civilian was burned.

The U.S. also sprayed the countryside with a chemical that accidentally harmed civilians as well as U.S. troops. This chemical was known as Agent Orange. It was designed to strip jungle plants of their leaves. Destroying the leafy cover made Vietcong guerrrillas easier to see and to attack from helicopter gunships. But Agent Orange caused cancer in some Vietnamese civilians and American service-

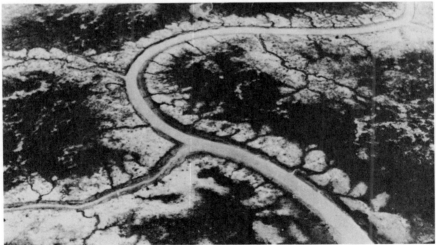

These photos dramatically illustrate the effects the herbicide Agent Orange had on the Vietnamese countryside. The top photo shows an airview of a river and the dense mangrove jungle surrounding it. The bottom photo shows a mangrove forest in 1970 that had been defoliated with Agent Orange five years earlier. The light spots are barren earth; the dark ones are some surviving trees.

Terrified children flee their village after it was bombed with napalm. One girl's burning clothes had to be torn off, forcing her to flee naked.

men who were exposed to it, and it often caused birth defects in their children.

The Vietcong and the North Vietnamese troops continued to receive military aid from China and the Soviet Union. The North Vietnamese were able to use antiaircraft guns and ground-to-air missiles to protect their cities from U.S. bombers. The Vietcong used hand-held rocket launchers to destroy U.S. helicopters. But the most effective weapon the Communists had did not come from China or the Soviet Union. It came from their ancestors; it was the knowledge of guerrilla warfare.

Just as they had killed the Chinese and the French soldiers with sneak attacks, the Vietnamese guerrillas began to kill many American troops in surprise raids. They also became expert in the use of hidden weapons, or booby traps. The Vietcong concealed thousands of land mines and grenades along jungle trails to kill or injure unsuspecting American soldiers.

One of the most feared Vietcong booby traps was the *punji* pit. The Vietcong made these by digging deep holes and placing sharpened bamboo stalks called *punji* sticks, in the soil at the bottom of the pits. They then covered the pits with sticks, leaves, and vines. When an American soldier stepped onto the thin covering, it gave way beneath him. He then fell onto the *punji* sticks, killing or injuring himself. *Punji* sticks were also hidden in mud balls and suspended above jungle trails to injure American soldiers who might unexpectedly walk into them.

Another deadly booby trap was the *dap loi*. To make a *dap loi*, the Vietcong filled an empty machine gun shell with gunpowder and bits of metal. They sealed a shell with wax and placed it in a bamboo tube with a nail pointing upwards below it. They buried the tube with the wax tip protruding slightly above the ground. When an American stepped on the shell, he pushed it down against the nail, which functioned like the hammer of a gun, igniting the gunpowder and blowing the metal into the soldier's foot.

The Vietcong also dug tunnels to fight U.S. soldiers. They sneaked in and out of villages through these tunnels and moved and stored supplies in them. American troops often would surround a Vietcong village, fight a fierce battle, sometimes destroy the entire village, only to find that the Vietcong had escaped through a tunnel.

The war drags on

The problems of the U.S. strategy together with the skill of the guerrilla warriors prolonged the war far beyond the time period the U.S. leaders and public expected. In November 1967, General Westmoreland told the American public and Congress, "The ranks

A mother and her baby peer out of a hole dug in the bank of a canal where they sought protection from a Vietcong attack on their village. They are discovered by a South Vietnamese soldier after the Vietcong retreat.

of the Vietcong are thinning steadily. . . .We have reached an important point when the end begins to come into view.'' But this was not the whole story. Privately, the general told President Johnson that if the U.S. continued fighting with the same number of forces, the war could go on indefinitely. Even with one hundred thousand additional troops, Westmoreland predicted, the war would last another three years.

The Tet Offensive

Less than three months after General Westmoreland told the American public the end of the war had come into view, the Vietcong launched an attack that cast serious doubt on the general's words. This attack came to be known as the Tet Offensive.

Tet marks the beginning of the Vietnamese New Year. Traditionally, the Vietnamese celebrate this holiday for several days. In honor of the holiday, the Vietcong, the South Vietnamese, and the Americans agreed to a brief truce. On January 30, 1968, most South Vietnamese troops were on holiday leave to celebrate Tet. In the warm light of their homes, the South Vietnamese laid down their rifles and raised their glasses to toast to success in the New Year. Voices joined in laughter and song. Fireworks crackled through the night. But the joyous popping of firecrackers was soon joined by another sound, the ominous "pop-pop-pop" of automatic rifle fire. The Vietcong were launching a surprise attack.

Guerrilla attacks

Under the direction of General Giap, the Vietcong struck hundreds of South Vietnamese towns, villages, and military bases. The guerrillas hoped to spark a popular uprising against the South Vietnamese government. They overran defenses across the country and executed hundreds of South Vietnamese government officials. Some of the heaviest fighting occurred in and around the old Vietnamese capital of Hue. Even the U.S. embassy in Saigon was occupied by the guerrilla forces.

U.S. troops bore the brunt of the attack, and they fought back bravely. Thousands of Vietcong were killed in the first waves of the offensive. U.S. and South Vietnamese troops joined forces to recapture most of the villages and towns that had been taken. The battles raged for days, from street to street, until the Vietcong were wiped out. The U.S. estimated that sixty thousand Vietcong and North Vietnamese troops took part in the Tet Offensive. Forty-five thousand died.

The Tet Offensive did not spark a popular revolt against the South Vietnamese government as the Vietcong had hoped it would. Nor did it result in a military victory for the Vietcong. But it did change the course of the war.

Despite the clear military victory for the U.S. that ended the Tet Offensive, many American leaders and citizens were shocked by the event. They found it hard to believe that the Vietcong had been able to move and coordinate so many troops. They were surprised to see villages and towns overrun by an enemy that was supposedly being defeated. U.S. military leaders had said the end of the war was in sight, like "the light at the end of the tunnel." After Tet, many Americans began to doubt their leaders. They feared that the darkest days still lay ahead.

CHAPTER FIVE

Why Did the United States Decide to Leave Vietnam? (1968-1972)

After the Tet Offensive, polls showed that a majority of Americans still supported the idea of winning the war, but a growing number believed the U.S. should get out of Vietnam. President Johnson's personal approval rating dropped from 48 percent to 36 percent. Only 26 percent of Americans approved of his handling of the war.

How could a win on the battlefield in Vietnam turn into a loss of support at home? There were several reasons.

The credibility gap

As the war progressed, many Americans stopped trusting their leaders. The fault was partly the government's. President Johnson had hurt his image by not being completely honest about American intentions in Vietnam.

During the 1964 presidential campaign, Johnson promised that "we are not about to send American boys nine or ten thousand miles away from home to do what Asian boys ought to be doing for themselves." A few months later, however, Johnson broke that promise by sending American troops into combat. Even then, the president waited a full month before informing the American people of this decision.

Before the 1968 Tet Offensive, Johnson ordered General

PRAIRIE STATE COLLEGE
LEARNING CENTER

3 2783 00005 2889

Westmoreland home from Vietnam to tell the American public the war was going well and an end was in sight. As the Tet Offensive raged, Johnson ordered Westmoreland to "reassure the public here that you have the situation under control."

Americans saw things differently on their television sets at home. Film of the Tet Offensive showed that Vietnam was a nation in turmoil, not a nation under control. Like someone who had caught a friend in a lie, Americans began to doubt that the government was being honest with them about the war. The gap between what the government said was happening and what people believed was happening was known as the credibility gap. The credibility gap did much to erode American support of the war in Vietnam.

The Johnson administration was not entirely to blame for its lack of credibility. Often the information the White House received from Vietnam was incomplete or simply wrong. When these mistakes were corrected, it appeared as though the government spokespeople were changing their stories. In addition, certain information could not be made public without endangering the soldiers fighting the war. But many people, especially those in the news media, believed that every time the government withheld information, it was hiding something bad.

The media and the war

Much of what Americans believed about the war came from what they saw on television. Many government officials believed these newscasts presented a distorted picture of the war. They believed that Americans were being misled about the war in Vietnam. The networks disagreed. They believed their coverage of the war was fair.

Whether the coverage was balanced or not, Americans simply were not used to seeing the horrors of war. When television brought it into their homes, they reacted against it. A single glimpse of a bloodied American soldier being dragged to safety by his buddies left a lasting impression.

As Americans became aware of the bloodshed in Vietnam, many began to protest against U.S. involvement. One focus of these protests was the draft. Because many troops were needed to fight the war, the U.S. military could not count on volunteers to fill its ranks. The government called for a draft of men who were eighteen years old or older. Some men responded by publicly burning their draft cards—identification cards issued to them by the Selective Service System. Antiwar protesters organized peace marches and sit-ins.

Many of the Vietnam protests were modeled after the peaceful civil rights demonstrations that had been led by Martin Luther King Jr. But as the war progressed, demonstrations against the war became more violent. Protesters occupied government and university buildings. They resisted police by throwing rocks and bottles. As antiwar turmoil spread across the nation, President Johnson's popularity declined.

David Wyatt, a student at the University of Washington, holds his burning draft card during a 1967 protest against Dow Chemical Company. Dow made napalm for use in the Vietnam War.

As President Johnson's support dwindled, those in his own party who opposed the war thought about challenging him in the presidential primaries. Primary elections allow members of each political party to select the candidate they most want to see run for president. The first Democrat to challenge President Johnson in a primary was Senator Eugene McCarthy of Minnesota. McCarthy entered the New Hampshire Democratic primary and campaigned on the theme of ending the war. President Johnson's name did not appear on the ballot because he had not officially entered the race. His supporters, however, mounted a write-in campaign on his behalf. When the results were counted in March 1968, McCarthy had lost the primary to the president by only three hundred votes of the fifty thousand votes that had been cast.

Robert Kennedy's platform

Four days after the New Hampshire primary, Robert Kennedy announced that he would seek the presidency. He also planned to run on a platform of ending the war. Faced with the growing opposition within his own party, President Johnson decided not to seek reelection. He announced that he would devote the remainder of his term to negotiating an end to the war. In May, leaders from North Vietnam and the United States met in Paris to begin talks aimed at ending the war.

Hubert Humphrey, Johnson's vice president, entered the Democratic race for the presidency. He and Robert Kennedy each won several primaries through the spring of 1968. In June 1968, however, Robert Kennedy was assassinated, and in August, Humphrey was nominated as the Democratic candidate for president.

Humphrey was opposed by the Republican nominee, Richard Nixon. Both candidates promised to end the war in Vietnam. Nixon claimed to have a secret plan to end the war. Humphrey offered to stop the bombing of North Vietnam and end American involvement in the war, a policy he called de-Americanization. In a matter of a

U.S. presidential adviser Henry Kissinger (right) and North Vietnamese negotiators Le Duc Tho (center) and Xuan Thuy wave encouragingly to the press. They have just come from a session of the 1973 Paris peace talks.

few months, the debate over Vietnam had changed completely. The question was no longer how the war could be won, but how best to end it.

The North Vietnamese leaders preferred Vice President Humphrey's plan. In Paris, they told American officials that a complete end of the bombing would produce results. Johnson, who was still president, was not sure what to do. He worried that if he stopped the bombing right before election day, he would be accused of using the war to help Humphrey get elected. But he did not want to allow a chance for peace to slip away. Finally, just one week before the election, he agreed to stop all bombing.

Johnson's decision helped Humphrey, but not enough to change the outcome of the election. Nixon edged out Humphrey by five hundred thousand votes, less than 1 percent of the total number of votes.

Vietnamization

Nixon planned to end the war, but he did not plan to abandon South Vietnam to the Communists. He believed that with American military and economic aid, the South Vietnamese could defend their country by themselves. He planned to withdraw American soldiers gradually, replacing them with well-trained, well-equipped Vietnamese soldiers. He called this plan Vietnamization.

Vietnamization was not a plan to end the war, but a way to end American involvement in the fighting. The war would continue, but it would be fought by South Vietnamese soldiers. Nixon told the American people, "We shall furnish military and economic assistance when requested in accordance with our treaty commitments. But we shall look to the nation directly threatened to assume the primary responsibility of providing the manpower for its defense."

In accordance with his plan for Vietnamization, Nixon announced the first withdrawal of American troops from Vietnam on June 8, 1969. Twenty-five thousand troops were sent home. By the end of the year, a total of sixty thousand American troops had been withdrawn.

Nixon also hoped to negotiate an end to the war itself. Five days after he took office, officials from the governments of the U.S., South Vietnam, and North Vietnam met in Paris to discuss the first serious peace proposals. The government of North Vietnam represented the Vietcong—the National Liberation Front (NLF). Members of the NLF also attended the talks, but they were not officially recognized as independent from the North Vietnamese. This condition was set by the government of South Vietnam. The South Vietnamese said they would not accept or attend the peace talks if the NLF was officially recognized.

The Paris peace talks did not produce results, however. Nixon stuck by President Johnson's old proposal that both the U.S. and North Vietnam withdraw their forces from South Vietnam at the same time. The North Vietnamese did not accept this proposal. They were not eager to end the war at a time when the U.S. seemed to be tiring of the effort. Better to wait for the U.S. to withdraw all its forces, then sweep through the south in a final assault.

Secret bombings

Nixon sensed that the North Vietnamese were trying to wait out the remaining time of U.S. involvement. He wanted to do something that would show the North Vietnamese that the U.S. was not going to allow a military takeover of South Vietnam. He knew that if he resumed the bombing of North Vietnam, the Communists would walk out of the Paris peace talks. This would make the U.S. look like it was not interested in peace. He decided to bomb North Vietnamese troops, but not to announce his decision to the press or the Congress.

After the 1968 Tet Offensive, the Vietcong had moved their head-quarters and supplies across the border of Vietnam, into Cambodia. The Vietcong bases were known as sanctuaries because they were located outside the fighting zone, in the neutral country of Cambodia. Since the Cambodian border lies within thirty miles of Saigon at its nearest point, the Vietcong were able to attack American troops, then retreat across the border. American troops were not allowed to cross the neutral border to strike back at the Communists. This gave the Vietcong an advantage that Nixon wanted to end.

Nixon knew that the North Vietnamese could not denounce the air strikes in Cambodia without admitting that they had moved troops into a neutral country. Early in 1969, he told the air force to bomb the sanctuaries. He also ordered that the bombings be kept secret from the American public and all but a few members of the U.S. Congress.

When information about the bombings became public, opponents of the war reacted strongly. Peace demonstrations were held across the U.S. Nixon was denounced for widening the war into a neutral country.

President Nixon reacted by speaking to the American people on television. He appealed to "the great silent majority" of Americans to support his policies. "Let us be united for peace," Nixon said. "Let us be united against defeat. Because let us understand: North Vietnam cannot defeat or humiliate the United States. Only Americans can do that."

A U.S. Skyraider swoops over the jungle and releases five-hundred-pound bombs on a Vietcong target below. Smoke rises from a previous hit. Air strikes were commonly used against the Vietcong.

After the speech, Nixon's popularity soared. But many people believed that the new president had also lost an important opportunity. Before this speech, Nixon could have ended U.S. involvement in Vietnam quickly, in almost any manner he wished. He could have taken credit for bringing home America's fighting troops and blamed any failure in Vietnam on his predecessor, Lyndon Johnson. By calling for the nation to unite behind him against defeat, Nixon assumed responsibility for the war. Johnson's war had become Nixon's war, and it would last another four years.

Leaks and wiretaps

At the same time that Nixon was publicly appealing to the American people for their support, he was also privately planning actions against certain Americans—the staff members and journalists he suspected of leaking the news about the secret bombings. The actions Nixon ordered would end by destroying his presidency and, ironically, destroying the South Vietnamese government he was trying to save with his secret bombings.

Nixon was furious that word about the secret bombings had leaked out of his administration and appeared in the news media in May 1969. Nixon and his national security advisor, Henry Kissinger, spoke

Richard M. Nixon, the only U.S. president to resign from office, gives his familiar victory sign as he leaves the White House for the last time on August 9, 1974.

with the director of the Federal Bureau of Investigation (FBI), J. Edgar Hoover, about placing listening devices on the phones of those who might have leaked the news. Shortly afterward, listening devices, known as wiretaps, were attached to the telephones of thirteen members of the Nixon administration and four journalists. Only the president and a few close aides knew about the wiretaps. It remained their secret for another four years.

Secret peace talks

President Nixon had hoped the bombing of Communist sanctuaries in Cambodia in 1969 would force North Vietnam to negotiate an end to the war. The bombing did not achieve this goal. The North Vietnamese leaders continued to demand that the new South Vietnamese president, Nguyen Van Thieu, resign. The Communists wanted to replace Thieu with a coalition government. A coalition is an alliance of persons, parties, or states. The coalition government would consist of members of Thieu's government and members of the NLF. President Nixon would not accept this proposal, but he did believe he could compromise with the North Vietnamese.

Forging such a compromise would require great honesty from both sides. Nixon did not believe that such forthrightness was possible in the Paris peace talks. Because such talks are conducted in front of countless journalists, the people involved in public negotiations sometimes hesitate to tell the entire truth. They are often afraid they will say the wrong thing in public. Nixon decided that the only way to end the war was through secret talks. He assigned Henry Kissinger the task of speaking directly with the leaders of North Vietnam.

In the early months of 1970, Kissinger began meeting with Le Duc Tho, an important person in the North Vietnamese government. Le Duc Tho had helped found the Indochinese Communist Party. He was in charge of Vietcong operations in South Vietnam. In short, he was the kind of top-level official with whom Nixon felt he could negotiate.

Kissinger and Tho continued to meet for two years. But while the secret talks went forward, so did the battle for South Vietnam.

Expanding the war

If the South Vietnamese were ever to hold their own against the Communists, they needed to stop the flow of North Vietnamese troops and supplies into their country. For many years, the North Vietnamese had sent men and materials into South Vietnam via the Ho Chi Minh Trail. This supply route wound through the mountains and jungles of Vietnam and the neutral countries of Laos and Cambodia. The Ho Chi Minh Trail was exactly that—a trail, not a highway or road. It was very difficult to see from the air and almost impossible to hit with bombs. Even if the trail was hit, the North Vietnamese simply carried their supplies around the bombed-out portion.

American bombings had failed to close the Ho Chi Minh Trail. The U.S. military, under the leadership of General Creighton Abrams, General Westmoreland's successor, saw only one other way to stop the flow of arms into the south. They wanted to send ground forces into Laos and Cambodia to close the trail. President Nixon approved.

In April 1970, U.S. and South Vietnamese forces invaded Cambodia, but the guerrillas proved to be as difficult as ever to find. The Communists retreated deep into Cambodia. The Americans and South Vietnamese were able to find and destroy large amounts of supplies, but they were unable to find the Vietcong headquarters located, they believed, just across the border.

Death at Kent State

Just as the bombing of Cambodia had sparked many protests in the U.S. a year before, the invasion of Cambodia touched off widespread demonstrations. At Kent State University in Ohio, opponents of the war attacked the campus building of the Reserve Officers' Training Corps (ROTC). Governor James Rhodes ordered the Ohio National Guard to break up the disturbance. Meeting

Nineteen-year-old William K. Schroeder, a student at Kent State University in Ohio, was shot and killed by Ohio National Guardsmen during an antiwar protest in May 1970.

resistance, the troops fired into the crowd. Four young people were killed.

The killings at Kent State shocked the American public. The fact that American military troops had used their weapons against unarmed American civilians seemed incredible to a nation that viewed its military and its government as servants of the people. Many Americans suddenly felt that something had gone terribly wrong with their country, and they poured into the streets in a new wave of demonstrations. Students and professors at more than four hundred colleges and universities refused to attend classes, shutting down the schools. Thousands of protesters flocked to Washington, D.C., to protest Nixon's policies and to show their support for the student demonstrators.

Members of the U.S. Senate also denounced the invasion of Cambodia. They proposed a law that would prevent further U.S. military action outside Vietnam. The law passed. The Senate also repealed the Gulf of Tonkin Resolution, the act passed in 1964 that gave the president authority to take all necessary measures against the Communist forces in Vietnam. Together, these votes marked the beginning of a new era in American foreign policy. Presidents would no longer enjoy so much power to send American troops to fight abroad without Congressional approval.

My Lai

Antiwar activity in the U.S. reached a high point after the invasion of Cambodia. But in the following months, the protests died down. As promised, American troop strength in Vietnam continued to shrink. By the end of 1970, only 280,000 troops were left in South Vietnam—down almost half from the high point just two years earlier. The number of American casualties decreased to five a week, the lowest number since 1965. South Vietnamese troops were indeed replacing Americans on the battlefront. The Vietcong, still recovering from their losses during the 1968 Tet Offensive, attacked less often. Relative calm settled over the U.S.—a calm that lasted until a storm of controversy swirled up around a young army lieutenant named William Calley.

The 1971 court-martial of Calley revealed that on the morning of March 16, 1968, he had ordered the troops under his command into the village of My Lai. Many Americans had been killed previously in and around My Lai by Vietcong guerrillas. As in countless other villages, the Vietcong in My Lai had enjoyed the support of many people. Fearful of the Americans, or simply longing for Vietnamese rule of any kind, the villagers had helped hide and supply the guerrillas. Once again, the American soldiers had faced the almost impossible task of distinguishing their enemies from the local residents. Lieutenant Calley had believed the situation called for decisive action.

All was quiet as Calley's troops surrounded the village: chickens pecked for grain in the dirt outside thatched huts; small children played; older children helped their mothers with chores. Suddenly, and without warning, the calm was broken. On Calley's signal, the American soldiers threw hand grenades into the huts. The Americans then shot the villagers who ran screaming from the huts. Mothers fell next to their children. Old bodies toppled over young. Calley himself herded dozens of villagers into a ditch and shot them. Between three hundred and five hundred unarmed civilians were killed.

Word about My Lai did not become public until 1969. When Calley was court-martialed, the media reported details of the testimony each day. Opponents of the war saw the massacre as further evidence of the immorality of American action. Many, however, saw Calley as a scapegoat, an individual singled out to bear the blame of many.

White tape marks off the area in the hamlet of My Lai where American soldiers killed Vietnamese civilians in 1968. The My Lai massacre was seen by many as a symbol of the immorality of U.S. involvement in Vietnam.

Army Lieutenant William Calley is escorted from his court-martial. He was found guilty of the premeditated murder of Vietnamese civilians.

Twenty-five soldiers had been charged with war crimes for their actions in My Lai, but only Calley had been convicted. To some, it seemed that Calley was being punished for the entire conduct of an immoral war.

A vocal critic gains support

By 1972, the war in Vietnam had reached an all-time low in popularity. During the Democratic primaries, voters turned away from their 1968 nominee, Hubert Humphrey, and voted heavily for an outspoken critic of the war, Senator George McGovern of South Dakota. McGovern's message was simple. He promised to end U.S. involvement in Vietnam within the first minutes of his presidency. He promised to take the oath of office at midnight of Inauguration Day and order all troops home immediately to ensure "not one more American would needlessly give his life to support a corrupt military dictatorship ten thousand miles away."

As the Democratic primaries moved from state to state, millions of Americans voted for the candidate who promised to get the U.S.

immediately out of Vietnam. McGovern believed the U.S. had already lost the battle for liberty in South Vietnam. "I have never felt that American interests or ideals were represented by the Saigon generals or their corrupt predecessors," McGovern declared in a statement before the U.S. Senate Committee on Foreign Relations. "The Saigon regime is an oppressive dictatorship which jails its critics and blocks the development of a broadly based government."

McGovern believed that the U.S. government was losing much more than the war itself. It had lost nearly fifty thousand young lives. It had lost the respect of many nations around the world. It had lost the confidence of millions of its own citizens. Most of all, McGovern believed, the U.S. had lost its hard-earned moral standing. "I find it morally and politically repugnant for us to create a client group of Vietnamese generals in Saigon, then give them murderous military technology to turn against their own people," McGovern said.

Despite his growing popularity, McGovern had a large number of critics, both inside his own party and among the Republicans. His critics pointed out that the rapid withdrawal of U.S. forces from Vietnam would almost certainly lead to a Communist victory in the south. They argued that while the South Vietnamese government might be flawed, Communist domination would be worse. This was the same lesser-of-two-evils logic that had guided U.S. foreign policy toward Vietnam for twenty-two years. McGovern responded, "The lesser of two evils is still evil."

The Spring Offensive

Sensing the growing American dissatisfaction with the war, the North Vietnamese decided the time had come for a new offensive in the south. By this time, two-thirds of the Communist forces in South Vietnam consisted of regulars from the North Vietnamese army. Their goal was to kill as many South Vietnamese soldiers as possible. They believed that these losses would discourage the South Vietnamese troops and would show the Americans that the South

Vietnamese could not defend themselves. They hoped this would convince American voters that Vietnamization was not working and that the U.S. should withdraw immediately. The Communists also believed they had nothing to fear from the U.S. They guessed that President Nixon would not send more American troops into combat during his reelection campaign.

Communist successes

The Communists attacked South Vietnamese positions across the country. Even though they lost fifty to seventy thousand troops, the North Vietnamese considered the Spring Offensive a success. For the first time, they had killed more troops than they had lost. They had captured large amounts of American-made military supplies. They had regained control of the many hamlets and villages they had lost in the Tet Offensive.

The Communists had correctly guessed that President Nixon would not respond to the offensive with increased American ground forces. The withdrawal of American combat forces continued throughout the presidential campaign. Instead, Nixon's response to the Spring Offensive came from the air. He ordered heavier bombing of North Vietnam.

American B-52s bombed the city of Haiphong for several days straight. A Soviet ship unloading supplies in the harbor was sunk. Water mines (bombs that float) were dropped into the harbor of Haiphong and other North Vietnamese ports.

U.S. bombs also fell on dikes in the Red River Delta. These dams, made of earth and wood, controlled the flooding of the Red River during the rainy season. Military estimates predicted that bombing the dikes would kill at least three hundred thousand civilians and destroy North Vietnam's main source of food. For years, the U.S. generals had urged that the dikes be targeted. Such civilian bombing had been routine in World War II. In Vietnam, however, bombing had been restricted to military targets, although many opponents of the war reported and believed civilian targets had been bombed. The

U.S. denied North Vietnamese reports that the dikes had been targeted, but Nixon's message was clear. Unless the Communist offensive ceased, the U.S. would destroy the dikes during the upcoming flood season.

Peace at hand

The North Vietnamese could not ignore this threat. They began to negotiate in earnest. In September 1972, they dropped their demand that President Thieu resign as president of South Vietnam. They agreed to allow the Saigon government to remain in power if an agreement could be reached. What they wanted, in exchange, was an in-

A South Vietnamese family in a slow-moving oxcart makes way for a column of American tanks. The tanks are headed north of Saigon to fight North Vietnamese in that area.

place cease-fire. This meant that after the fighting stopped, all Vietnamese troops would stay where they were. U.S. troops would leave Vietnam, but the North Vietnamese soldiers would not have to leave the south. They and the South Vietnamese army would remain in place.

In October, Kissinger and Le Duc Tho reached an agreement on a cease-fire. On October 21, the government of North Vietnam approved the treaty. Kissinger flew to South Vietnam to get President Thieu's approval.

Further negotiations needed

Thieu would not accept the terms of the treaty. He refused to allow North Vietnamese troops to remain on South Vietnamese soil. Kissinger informed President Nixon of the situation and returned home. Nixon realized that the agreement could not be completed before the election. He told Kissinger to notify the North Vietnamese that further negotiations would be needed.

On October 24, President Thieu publicly denounced the treaty. The North Vietnamese responded by making the terms of the treaty public and accusing the U.S. of trying to back out of the agreement. In Washington, Kissinger met with reporters. He did not want the American public to think he had negotiated a treaty that was unfair to the South Vietnamese. Rather, he wanted Americans to believe that only a few details needed to be worked out before peace would be possible. He told the reporters, "We believe that peace is at hand. We believe that an agreement is within sight." The next day, newspapers across the country carried the headline "Peace at Hand."

A few days later, Americans went to the polls to elect a president. Thirty-eight million people voted for McGovern and an immediate end to the war. But the vast majority of voters preferred Nixon's policy of peace with honor. Nixon won nearly 60 percent of the vote. He carried every state in the union except Massachusetts.

After the election, the peace talks in Paris resumed, but the U.S.

was no longer willing to accept an in-place cease-fire. Once more, the U.S. insisted that the North Vietnamese agree to withdraw from the south. North Vietnam was willing to compromise on small matters, but not on this large issue. On December 13, the talks broke down completely. Le Duc Tho returned to Hanoi.

The next day, President Nixon warned the North Vietnamese that if they did not return to the peace talks, he would again bomb their cities. The North Vietnamese refused.

One week before Christmas, U.S. B-52s and other aircraft began to bomb North Vietnam. The bombing lasted until December 30, with a one-day pause on Christmas Day. Americans flew more than three thousand missions, dropping more than forty thousand tons of bombs. It was the most intensive bombing since the end of World War II. Still, the number of civilian casualties was quite small compared with civilian casualties in World War II, according to Stanley Karnow, author of *Vietnam, A History*. Karnow wrote, ''The official North Vietnamese figure for civilian fatalities for the period was 1,318 in Hanoi and 305 in Haiphong—hardly the equivalent of the Americans' incendiary bombing of Tokyo in March 1945, for example, when nearly eighty-four thousand people were killed in a single night.''

The U.S. lost twenty-six aircraft in the raids. Thirty-one pilots and crew members became prisoners of war. Sixty-two died. But these were among the last Americans to lose their lives in Vietnam. During the bombings, the North Vietnamese agreed to talk. On January 8, 1973, Kissinger and Le Duc Tho met again in Paris. The next day, they agreed to a settlement. For this, Kissinger and Tho were awarded the 1973 Nobel Peace Prize. More importantly, after nearly twenty-three years, American involvement in Vietnam was about to end.

CHAPTER SIX

Why Did South Vietnam Fall?

Many Americans were pleased when the U.S. signed the Paris Peace Treaty on January 27, 1973. But the treaty did not mean good news for the government of South Vietnam. The U.S. had agreed to nearly the same conditions President Thieu had rejected three months before. The North Vietnamese would be allowed to stay in the south. In this sense, the Christmas bombings had accomplished nothing.

This time, South Vietnam agreed to the treaty, mainly because Nixon gave Thieu no choice. He told the South Vietnamese leader that the U.S. would sign the agreement with or without Thieu's approval. He also promised Thieu that the U.S. would "respond with full force should the settlement be violated by North Vietnam." He also offered to replace every plane, tank, rifle, and bullet the South Vietnamese might lose in future battles with the Communists. Thieu did not want to risk losing American economic and military aid, so he agreed to these terms.

The last American combat forces had left Vietnam on March 29, 1973, although several thousand military advisors remained. Since the treaty did not apply to territory outside Vietnam, the U.S. continued to bomb the Ho Chi Minh Trail in Cambodia to prevent more North Vietnamese troops and materials from reaching the south.

Even though President Nixon was determined to help the South Vietnamese government, the U.S. Congress was not. With the American troops home at last, the Congress saw little reason to continue spending money in Vietnam. In June, the Congress passed a bill that cut off funding for all military operations in Indochina. President Nixon fought for the right to intervene in Vietnam in the event of a Communist attack, but Congress ignored Nixon's pleas. Although he had been reelected by a landslide just months before, Nixon had lost his ability to influence Congress. By the summer of 1973, the Watergate hearings had opened in Washington, and members of Congress were beginning to question Nixon's ability to lead the country.

Watergate

The event that led to the Watergate investigation occurred during the 1972 presidential campaign. Five men were arrested for breaking into the Democratic National Headquarters in the Watergate Hotel in Washington, D.C., and attempting to place wiretaps on the telephones. It soon became clear that this break-in was not due to the zeal of a few isolated supporters of the president. Hearings revealed that the defendants were linked to the Committee to Reelect the President (CREEP), which was headed by members of the Nixon administration.

The Watergate case sparked a Congressional investigation into secret White House operations. A select Senate subcommittee discovered that the Nixon administration had created an enemies list and engaged in illegal activities that went all the way back to the 1969 wiretaps placed on phones after news of the secret bombing of Cambodia had been leaked to the press.

Nixon's handling of the Watergate affair led to a crisis in American government. For months, the administration maintained its innocence and refused to cooperate with investigations into its activities. Nixon ordered his aides to tell as little as possible about White House operations. He instructed staff members to say that they "did not

As his wife Pat looks on, President Richard Nixon makes an emotional farewell speech to his White House staff before leaving office on August 9, 1974.

remember'' and ''did not recall'' secret activities. In July 1974, the Supreme Court ordered the White House to turn over tape recordings of Nixon's conversations to the special prosecutor appointed to investigate the Watergate case. A few days later, the Judiciary Committee of the House of Representatives approved three articles of impeachment to remove Nixon from office. Rather than stand trial before the Senate, Nixon chose to resign from office, and he did resign on August 9, 1974.

The Watergate scandal seriously weakened the administration Nixon left behind. Nixon's successor was Vice President Gerald Ford. Like Nixon, he was unable to convince Congress to support the South Vietnamese government in the event of Communist aggression—an event that was to come soon.

The Communists were prepared to wait years before moving their forces against the South Vietnamese government, but events in the U.S. convinced them that they could act sooner. In the spring of 1975, they launched what was to be the final offensive of the Vietnam War.

The South Vietnamese generals had stationed most of their troops near the border that divided North and South Vietnam. In the event of war, they expected the North Vietnamese to sweep across the Demilitarized Zone (DMZ), an area on either side of the border between North and South Vietnam. According to the 1954 Geneva Ac-

A tank provides cover as soldiers try to force out Communist troops holed up in the ancient citadel at Hue, the old capital of Vietnam. Hue fell to Communist troops soon after American troops withdrew from Vietnam.

A small party of U.S. Marines waits tensely behind the crumbled walls of the old fortress at Hue. They await the next attack by Vietcong guerrillas who are gathering in the demolished buildings below.

cords and the 1973 Paris Peace Treaty, this area was to be kept free of military troops and equipment.

Once more, the Communists outsmarted the South Vietnamese army. They secretly moved 150,000 troops into the central provinces of South Vietnam. In December 1974, the Communists attacked. By January 6, 1975, they had captured Phuoc Binh, the capital of Phuoc Long province.

Next, the North Vietnamese moved northward against the forces in the central highlands around Pleiku and Kontum. Foreseeing disaster, President Thieu ordered his troops to retreat to the southern part of Vietnam. The Communists shelled the retreating troops. Thousands of South Vietnamese soldiers died in what some experts have called the most poorly planned military retreat in history.

Surprised with the ease of their conquests, the North Vietnamese pushed on. On March 25, the city of Hue fell to the Communists. Thousands of civilians and South Vietnamese troops fled to Da Nang, South Vietnam's second largest city. The Communists quickly surrounded the city. Five days later, 100,000 South Vietnamese troops surrendered.

Within two weeks, the North Vietnamese had conquered half of Vietnam. They had killed or captured one-third of the South Vietnamese army. In Da Nang, they had captured more than one billion dollars worth of American military supplies. The leaders of North Vietnam decided to push on toward Saigon. They hoped to capture the South Vietnamese capital before the rainy season began in May.

The fall of Saigon

The U.S. ambassador, Graham Martin, urged Congress to send more money to South Vietnam. Martin believed that with more money, the South Vietnamese might be able to stop the Communist advance. Henry Kissinger, secretary of state under President Ford, appeared before the Senate to appeal for funds. Congress was unmoved by Kissinger's arguments. After more than a quarter-century of support, the U.S. was cutting South Vietnam loose. The South Vietnamese would have to fight the North Vietnamese on their own.

By April 9, 1975, the Communist forces had advanced to within forty miles of Saigon. The South Vietnamese army made a valiant last stand at a small town called Xuan Loc. There, five thousand South Vietnamese soldiers held off nearly forty thousand North Vietnamese for twelve days. On April 21, however, the Communists overran Xuan Loc.

More than one hundred thousand North Vietnamese troops surrounded Saigon. The South Vietnamese government had only thirty thousand troops left to defend the city. President Thieu resigned and left the country. The remaining Americans and thousands of South Vietnamese prepared to join him. Many left by plane. On April 29, the Communists began shelling the Saigon airport. The only option left was to evacuate by helicopter.

Americans were informed of the evacuation by a prearranged, secret signal. A Saigon radio station began playing Bing Crosby's recording of "White Christmas" every fifteen minutes. The remaining Americans and thousands of Vietnamese civilians rushed toward landing sites on the tops of buildings and within the U.S. embassy compound.

Americans and other foreigners line up to board an evacuation helicopter atop a government building in Saigon in April 1975. Saigon was about to fall into the hands of the North Vietnamese Communist forces.

Seventy helicopters flew into Saigon from American ships anchored off the coast of Vietnam. American troops spilled out of the choppers. They had returned to Vietnam not to fight, but to protect the evacuation sites. Flying back and forth between Saigon and the American ships, the helicopters removed the one thousand remaining Americans and six thousand Vietnamese civilians, many of whom had worked for the U.S. government.

The flights continued all night long. Many hysterical South Vietnamese civilians tried to bribe or force their way onto the helicopters. At dawn on April 30, 1975, the last U.S. helicopters left the embassy compound. Ambassador Martin and his wife boarded one of the last choppers. Under his arm, the ambassador carried his embassy's American flag.

Later that day, the Communists marched into the heart of Saigon. They promptly renamed the southern capital Ho Chi Minh City, after the leader who had begun the struggle to remove the foreigners from his land more than thirty years before.

Epilogue

Many experts predicted that if the Communists gained control of Vietnam, a bloodbath would follow. After the 1968 Tet Offensive, the Vietcong had executed more than three thousand civilian officials in the city of Hue alone. After the fall of Saigon in 1975, however, no bloodbath occurred. But the fighting and misery were not yet over for the Vietnamese.

Once the Communists gained control of South Vietnam, millions of South Vietnamese civilians were forced from the cities into reeducation camps. The camps were designed to teach people the basic principles of communism, mainly that working for the good of all is better than working for personal gain. No matter what education or skills these civilians possessed, they were forced to do simple labor. Instead of performing the duties they were trained for, doctors, dentists, nurses, and teachers were sent into the countryside to grow rice.

Continued turmoil

Vietnam was unified into one country, known as the Socialist Republic of Vietnam. But the peace achieved by this unification did not last long. During their retreat into Cambodia in 1970, the Vietcong had led an uprising of the Cambodian people against the Cambodian government. The fighting between various rebel groups had continued for years. Frequently, the Cambodians clashed with the Vietnamese along the border. On December 28, 1978, the Vietnamese soldiers invaded Cambodia. Eventually, they gained control of the entire country; more lives were lost.

Hundreds of thousands of refugees fled from the Vietnamese in Cambodia and Laos. Most of these refugees poured into Malaysia and Thailand. Many remained homeless.

The Chinese supported the existing government in Cambodia, and they were not pleased when the Vietnamese invaded. In early 1979, the Chinese retaliated by invading the northernmost regions of Vietnam. Although the fighting lasted only a few weeks, both the Vietnamese and the Chinese suffered thousands of casualties. Tension between the two nations continues today.

Refugees

Because of the Chinese invasion, the Vietnamese government forced more than four hundred thousand ethnic Chinese—Vietnamese people with Chinese ancestors—to leave Vietnam. Their businesses were closed. They were often required to pay large fees before leaving the country. The Vietnamese-Chinese refugees often fled aboard small ships and fishing boats. The boat people, as they were called, had no idea about where to go. Hundreds of thousands have been taken in by countries in Asia and Europe, and by the United States. In America, the Vietnamese have taken their place beside the many other immigrants that have come to the U.S. in the twentieth century: the Irish, Germans, Poles, Russian Jews, Mexicans, Cubans, Nicaraguans, Haitians, and Salvadorans.

Vietnam veterans

Vietnamese refugees are not the only Americans whose lives changed dramatically after the Vietnam War. The lives of the Vietnam veterans changed, too. For many, arriving in the U.S. was like arriving in a foreign land. Americans had always honored their war heroes, but this time many Americans shunned them.

Some Americans reacted with fear to Vietnam veterans. Average civilians had heard of widespread drug abuse in Vietnam. They had heard of atrocities in the war—soldiers going crazy and turning their weapons on innocent civilians. When many Vietnam veterans walked the streets of their home towns, friends and family often treated them as if they were insane, ready to blow up at any moment.

Like veterans of all wars, many Vietnam veterans did suffer mental troubles after the war. The problem, called post-traumatic stress disorder, sometimes caused veterans to act violently. When the media reported these stories across the U.S., it further confirmed the image many Americans held of the crazed Vietnam veteran.

Some veterans were not surprised by the cold reception they received. The war had been unpopular—the most unpopular war in American history. Surely those who fought the war would be just as unpopular.

Many veterans suspected that their treatment would have been different had the U.S. won the war. Facing its first defeat on the battlefield, the U.S. was looking for someone to blame. It was as if many Americans decided to blame the soldiers for losing the war.

A group of Vietnam veterans gathers on a Chicago street in March 1989 to protest an art exhibit they perceive to be disrespectful to the American flag.

Slowly, the attitudes of many Americans toward the Vietnam vets are changing. In part, this is due to the outpouring of motion pictures and books about Vietnam. *Going After Cacciato*, a novel about Vietnam by Tim O'Brien, who served as a foot soldier in Vietnam, won a National Book Award in 1978. In 1983, the PBS television network showed a thirteen-part documentary called ''Vietnam: A Television History,'' which, along with the companion book by Stanley Karnow, reached millions of American homes. The movie *Platoon* won the Academy Award for Best Picture in 1987. Other motion pictures, including *Apocalypse Now, The Deer Hunter, Coming Home, Good Morning, Vietnam*, and *Full Metal Jacket*, have each shed light on many different facets of the war. In the late 1980s, two television series, ''Tour of Duty'' and ''China Beach,'' attempted to show the soldiers' views of the war.

Veterans contribute to America's understanding

The Vietnam veterans themselves have contributed to an understanding of the war that did not exist when they first returned to the U.S. Some veterans have toured high school and college campuses to speak about the war. They have shared their stories and discussed their feelings, both about the war and about the rejection they met when they came home. This has helped not only those who have heard the veterans, but also the veterans themselves. For many, being able to talk about the war has been a great relief.

On Veterans Day, November 11, 1982, the Vietnam Veterans Memorial was dedicated in Washington, D.C. This wall of polished black granite, inscribed with the names of all the soldiers who died or are missing in Vietnam, has helped bring together those who served in Vietnam and those whom they served. The wall that commemorates America's losses has helped replace the wall of misunderstanding that stood between many Americans and their veterans.

Although Americans have learned to respect the veterans who fought in Vietnam, they have not agreed on the lessons to be learned

A family of Vietnamese "boat people" smiles with relief as they arrive safely at their new home in Des Moines, Iowa.

from the struggle. Opinion polls have shown that feelings about the war have changed little in the years since it was fought. Those who supported it still tend to believe the war should have been fought— and won. Those who opposed the war still believe it was wrong.

Public loses confidence in the war

According to many experts, one of the main problems with the war was the fact that the American public did not fully support American military involvement. Once the public lost confidence in the war, the effort was doomed. Some people blame President Johnson for not declaring war in 1964. One such person is Colonel Harry G. Sumners, a former infantry officer in Vietnam. As a staff member at the Army War College in Carlisle, Pennsylvania, Sumners wrote, "A . . . declaration of war makes the prosecution of the war a shared responsibility of both the government and the American people. . . . The failure to declare war in Vietnam drove a wedge between the Army and large segments of the American public.''

Others believe the American failure had more to do with what happened on the battleground than what occurred at home. John Mueller, a professor of political science at the University of Rochester in Rochester, New York, argued that the U.S. could not have known that ''the Communist side was willing to accept battle death rates that were twice as high as those accepted by the fanatical, often suicidal Japanese in World War II.'' Dean Rusk, secretary of state under Presidents Kennedy and Johnson, agreed with this view. In 1971, he stated that American leaders ''underestimated the resistance and determination of the North Vietnamese.''

Some believe the war might have turned out differently if the U.S. military had simply followed a different strategy. Norman Hannah, a retired foreign service officer, believes the problem came when the U.S. decided to fight the Vietcong in the south rather than cut off the supply of men and material from North Vietnam. Others believe the U.S. should have actually invaded North Vietnam and driven Ho Chi Minh out of Hanoi.

A completely foreign land

Many people believe the central problem in Vietnam was the failure to recognize the great differences that exist between the peoples of the world. Vietnam was more than a difficult place for Americans to do battle. It was an entirely different culture, one the U.S. never understood. Instead of acting out a power struggle against the Soviet Union, the U.S. should have looked realistically at the wants and needs of the Vietnamese people. This might have kept the U.S out of Vietnam in the first place.

Certainly the deciding factor in the war was the support the Vietcong received from the people. Whether the Vietnamese peasants really longed for Communist rule or whether they simply wanted independence, they never supported the governments that the U.S. supported in South Vietnam. Without support of the Vietnamese people, the American effort was futile.

Perhaps the final legacy of Vietnam for the U.S. will be an attitude of greater caution in committing troops around the globe. The U.S. probably will not shrink into a shell, deciding never again to send its fighting forces abroad. But because of Vietnam, American leaders have been and will probably continue to be more cautious about getting involved in foreign conflicts. If they do decide to commit American troops abroad, they will probably want to make sure they have the support of the Congress, the support of the people, and the weight of world opinion on their side.

Glossary

Agent Orange Chemical sprayed on jungle foliage by U.S. forces to strip the plants of their leaves, thus making the enemy more visible.

bloc Nations with a common interest or purpose who form a unit.

boat people South Vietnamese of Chinese ancestry who were forced to leave Vietnam by boat, seeking refuge in other countries.

capitalism An economic system that depends on the unlimited ownership of property and investments and on competition in the free market to determine means of production and distribution of goods.

colonialism Control by one power over a dependent area or people.

communism An economic system that eliminates the ownership and distribution of private property. Investments, production and distribution of goods, and prices are all state-controlled.

containment Policy first advocated by President Harry Truman to hold back the spread of communism throughout the world.

coup d'état The violent overthrow of a government.

credibility gap The difference between what the U.S. government told the American people was happening during the Vietnam War and what the people believed was happening.

dap loi Vietcong booby trap consisting of a machine gun shell filled with gunpowder and bits of metal. The end of the shell is filled with wax and placed in a bamboo tube with a nail pointing upwards below it. The tube is then buried with the wax protruding slightly above the ground. When the wax is stepped on, the shell explodes.

domino theory Theory that as Communists gain control of countries in one area, those countries will topple the governments in other countries that share their borders.

draft Compulsory enrollment of people into military service.

escalation Increase in number or intensity, as in sending more soldiers to fight a war.

Geneva Accords Agreement reached in 1954 at a conference in Geneva, Switzerland that divided North and South Vietnam.

guerrilla warfare Fighting by troops that are not members of a regular army. Military strategy involves surprise attacks and hasty retreats before the enemy can respond.

Gulf of Tonkin Resolution Act passed in 1964 that gave the president of the United States ultimate authority to take all necessary measures against Communist forces in Vietnam. The resolution was repealed in 1970.

hamlet Small village.

Ho Chi Minh Trail Trail that winds through the mountains and jungles of Vietnam, Laos, and Cambodia by which the North Vietnamese sent soldiers and supplies into South Vietnam.

Indochina Asian countries of Burma, Thailand, Cambodia, Laos, Malaysia, and Vietnam.

isolationism Belief that one's country should not become involved in the affairs of other countries.

napalm bomb Bomb that contains a sticky substance that ignites as quickly as gasoline.

pacification System used by the French in Vietnam to ensure French control of villages located in the war zone. It involved punishing villagers for helping the Vietminh and protecting the villagers from attack.

primary election Preliminary election in which a Republican and a Democratic candidate are chosen to run in the final election.

punji **pit** Vietcong booby trap consisting of a deep hole containing sharpened bamboo sticks (*punji* sticks) that stand upright in the soil at the bottom of the pit. The pits are covered with sticks, leaves, and vines and are difficult to detect. A person who falls into a *punji* pit is often killed or wounded by the *punji* sticks.

reeducation camps Political camps run by the North Vietnamese after they gained control of Vietnam. The camps were designed to teach the South Vietnamese people the basic principles of communism.

Rolling Thunder President Johnson's campaign of continuous bombing of Vietnam.

sanctuary Vietcong military base located in Cambodia outside the fighting zone.

search and destroy mission Combat mission in which American troops searched for villages controlled by the Vietcong and destroyed their supplies.

seventeenth parallel   Horizontal line that divides North Vietnam from South Vietnam.

Spring Offensive   Communist attacks across South Vietnam in 1972 to convince the Americans that the South Vietnamese were unable to defend themselves.

strategic hamlet program   Moving of Vietnamese citizens out of their homes and into hamlets, or small villages, to separate them from the Vietcong.

Tet Offensive   Surprise attack on South Vietnam by the Vietcong during the Vietnamese New Year's truce in 1968.

United Nations   International organization of nations formed in 1945 to pursue world peace.

Viet Bac   Area from which the Vietminh attacked South Vietnamese and U.S. forces located in the Red River Delta.

Vietcong   Communist Vietnamese located in South Vietnam.

Vietminh   Name of the Vietnam Independence League that was formed by Ho Chi Minh to resist Japanese and French occupation of Vietnam. The Vietminh forces later fought U.S. and South Vietnamese forces in South Vietnam.

Vietnamization   President Nixon's plan to withdraw American troops from South Vietnam gradually and replace them with equipped and trained South Vietnamese soldiers.

war of attrition   A war whose strategy involves reducing the number of enemies, usually by killing them, rather than conquering land.

Watergate investigation   An investigation of members of the Nixon administration after they broke into the Democratic National Headquarters in the Watergate Hotel in 1972.

Chronology of U.S. Involvement in Vietnam

June 27, 1950 President Truman sends military personnel to Vietnam to aid French forces.

December 23, 1950 The United States, France, Vietnam, Cambodia, and Laos sign the Mutual Defense Assistance Agreement to protect Southeast Asia from Communist invasion.

November 1952 Dwight Eisenhower is elected president of the United States.

May 7, 1954 Vietminh forces defeat French forces at Dien Bien Phu.

July 21, 1954 Geneva Accords call for cease-fire in Vietnam and divide the country into North Vietnam and South Vietnam.

January 1, 1955 The United States begins to send aid directly to the South Vietnamese government.

May, 1959 U.S. advisors are ordered to Vietnam to assist South Vietnamese infantry, artillery, and naval forces.

November 1960 John F. Kennedy is elected president of the United States.

May 5, 1961 President Kennedy announces it may be necessary to send U.S. troops to Vietnam.

May 1, 1963 Buddhists gather in the city of Hue to protest a decree against flying their flag. Ngo Dinh Diem's troops fire into the crowd, killing eight children and one woman.

November 1, 1963 Military coup overthrows Ngo Dinh Diem's government, killing Diem and his brother, Ngo Dinh Nhu.

November 22, 1963 President Kennedy is assassinated. Lyndon Johnson becomes president.

August 2, 1964 U.S. warship *Maddox* is attacked in the Gulf of Tonkin.

August 3, 1964 U.S. Senate votes in favor of the Gulf of Tonkin Resolution allowing President Johnson to bypass Congress and take all necessary measures to protect U.S. forces in Southeast Asia.

November 1964 Lyndon Johnson is elected president of the United States.

February 7, 1965 President Johnson orders bombing of North Vietnam after American soldiers are killed in a Vietcong attack.

July 25, 1965 President Johnson addresses the American people on television and determines that U.S. troops will remain in Vietnam.

April 15, 1967 One hundred thousand people in the United States demonstrate against the Vietnam War.

January 30, 1968 The Vietcong launch a surprise attack, called the Tet Offensive, against South Vietnam during the Vietnamese New Year's truce.

November 1968 Richard Nixon is elected president of the United States.

March 18, 1969 President Nixon orders secret bombing in Cambodia.

June 8, 1969 President Nixon announces first U.S. troop withdrawal from Vietnam, in accordance with his plan for Vietnamization.

September 3, 1969 Ho Chi Minh dies.

November 3, 1969 President Nixon appeals to the silent majority to support his policy of peace with honor.

November 12, 1969 U.S. Army announces alleged killings of civilians by U.S. troops in March of 1968 in My Lai.

February 20, 1970 Peace talks begin in Paris between Henry Kissinger and Le Duc Tho.

April 29, 1970 U.S. and South Vietnamese invade Cambodia to attack North Vietnamese and Vietcong sanctuaries.

May 4, 1970 Ohio national guardsmen kill four Kent State University students during anti-war demonstration.

June 24, 1970 U.S. Senate repeals 1964 Gulf of Tonkin Resolution.

March 29, 1971 Lt. William Calley is convicted of murdering South Vietnamese civilians at My Lai.

Spring 1972 Communist forces attack South Vietnam during the Spring Offensive.

May 8, 1972 President Nixon orders heavy bombing of North Vietnam. Water mines are dropped into the harbor at Haiphong and other North Vietnamese ports.

September 1972   North Vietnam and U.S. begin earnest negotiations for a cease-fire.

October 21, 1972   Henry Kissinger and Le Duc Tho reach a cease-fire agreement.

October 24, 1972   President Nguyen Van Thieu denounces the cease-fire agreement reached by Kissinger and Tho.

December 13, 1972   Paris peace talks break down completely.

December 1972   U.S. B-52s and other aircraft bomb North Vietnam.

January 27, 1973   Cease-fire agreement signed in Paris.

March 29, 1973   Last U.S. troops leave Vietnam.

August 9, 1974   President Nixon resigns as a result of the Watergate scandal. Gerald Ford becomes president.

Spring 1975   North Vietnamese launch the final offensive of the Vietnam War, capturing half of Vietnam and killing or capturing one-third of the South Vietnamese army.

April 30, 1975   Saigon falls to the Communists; remaining Americans in Vietnam are evacuated.

November 11, 1982   Vietnam Veterans Memorial is dedicated in Washington, D.C.

Major Figures in the Vietnam War

William Calley   Lieutenant in the U.S. army held responsible for the My Lai massacre.

Ngo Dinh Diem   Leader of South Vietnam from 1954-1963; Diem's intolerance of the religious and political beliefs of his people enraged Vietnamese citizens. He was killed by his own generals in 1963.

John Foster Dulles   U.S. secretary of state from 1953-1959; Dulles supported French involvement in Vietnam.

Dwight D. Eisenhower   U.S. president from 1953-1961; Eisenhower agreed to help France retain control of Vietnam, but he stipulated that France must agree to eventually liberate Vietnam.

Gerald R. Ford   U.S. president from 1974-1976, after Nixon's resignation; Ford was unable to convince Congress to give further support to South Vietnam.

Vo Nguyen Giap   Commander of the Communist forces that defeated the French at Dien Bien Phu; Giap continued as chief Communist strategist in the war against the United States and South Vietnam.

Hubert Humphrey   Vice president under Lyndon Johnson from 1964-1968; Humphrey ran for president against Richard Nixon in 1968, losing by less than 1 percent of the total votes.

Lyndon Johnson   U.S. president from 1963-1968; responding to the North Vietnamese attack on the U.S. warship *Maddox*, Johnson sent thousands of U.S. troops to Vietnam. He ordered the continuous bombing, known as Rolling Thunder, of Vietnam.

John F. Kennedy   U.S. president from 1960-1963; Kennedy was concerned that Ngo Dinh Diem did not have the support of the Vietnamese people and that democracy could not be won in Vietnam without this support. He repeatedly warned Diem to show more tolerance toward Vietnamese citizens. Kennedy was assassinated three weeks after Diem, in November 1963.

Robert Kennedy   U.S. attorney general in his brother John's administration; he served as senator from New York from 1965-1968. He ran as a democratic presidential candidate in 1968 but was assassinated in June of that year.

Henry Kissinger   National security adviser under Richard Nixon from 1969-1973; Kissinger negotiated with Le Duc Tho until the Paris Peace Settlement was reached in 1973. Kissinger and Tho were awarded the Nobel Peace Prize in 1973 for this accomplishment. Nixon later appointed Kissinger secretary of state, a position he held from 1973-1977.

Henry Cabot Lodge   U.S. ambassador to Vietnam from 1963-1964 and again from 1965-1967; he approved the overthrow of Ngo Dinh Diem's government.

George McGovern   U.S. senator from South Dakota and presidential candidate in 1972; during the primary election, McGovern promised to end U.S. involvement in Vietnam within the first minutes of his presidency. He won the primary but lost the election to Richard Nixon.

Ho Chi Minh   President of North Vietnam from 1945 until his death in 1969; he left Vietnam and moved to Paris in 1917, where he joined the French Communist Party in 1920. In 1941, he returned to Vietnam where he formed the Vietminh. His troops fought the French from 1945-1954. His troops defeated the French at Dien Bien Phu in May 1954.

Richard Nixon   Vice president under Dwight D. Eisenhower from 1952-1961; Nixon lost the presidential campaign to John F. Kennedy in 1960, but he won out over Hubert Humphrey in the 1968 campaign. He defeated George McGovern in the 1972 election. He was forced to resign in August 1974 after the Watergate investigation.

Nguyen Van Thieu   President of South Vietnam from 1967-1973; Thieu fled Vietnam just before the fall of Saigon in April 1975.

Le Duc Tho   Founder of the Indochinese Communist Party and leader of the North Vietnamese army; he and Henry Kissinger were awarded the Nobel Peace Prize for achieving a cease-fire agreement in January 1963. Tho rejected the award.

Harry S. Truman   As president of the United States from 1945-1952, Truman ordered the first American soldiers to go to Vietnam to help the French in their battle for control of the country. He initiated the containment policy to hold back the spread of communism.

William Westmoreland   Commander of U.S. combat forces in Vietnam from 1964-1968; he later became chief of staff of the army. Westmoreland initiated a war of attrition against the Vietcong, which meant killing as many of the enemy as possible.

Suggestions for Further Reading

Ray Bonds, *The Vietnam War*. New York: Crown, 1979.

Joseph Buttinger, *Vietnam: The Unforgettable Tragedy*. New York: Horizon Press, 1977.

Wendy Cole, *Vietnam*. New York: Chelsea House, 1989.

Ernest Barksdale Fincher, *The Vietnam War*. New York: Franklin Watts, 1980.

J. Greenwald, "The Wound That Will Not Heal," *Time*, October 10, 1988.

Denis J. Hauptley, *In Vietnam*. New York: Atheneum, 1985.

Paul Hensler, *Don't Cry, It's Only Thunder*. Garden City, NY: Doubleday, 1984.

Stanley Karnow, *Vietnam: A History*. New York: Viking, 1983.

Don Lawson, *The War in Vietnam*. New York: Franklin Watts, 1981.

P. Vespa, "His Dream Was to Heal a Nation . . .," *People Weekly*, May 30, 1988.

P. Witeman, "Welcome Back to Vietnam," *Time*, January 18, 1988.

Index

Picture Credits

Photos supplied by Dixon and Turner Research Associates, Inc.,
 Bethesda, MD

Cover photo reprinted with permission of Blackstar/Christopher Mowro
AP/Wide World Photos, 8, 13, 16, 17, 22, 24, 25, 27, 31, 32, 33, 35, 43, 51,
 53, 56, 60, 62, 63, 65, 72, 73, 79, 81
Mary Arndt, 12
UPI/Bettmann Newsphotos, 39, 40, 44, 46, 57, 66, 71, 75

About the Author

Harry Nickelson is an artist whose work is shown throughout the Los Angeles area. He also writes poetry, has had several poems published, and is currently writing two children's books.

Mr. Nickelson's interest in Vietnam began during his last years of high school when he was required to register for the draft. Although U.S. involvement in Vietnam ended before he was drafted, his interest in why the U.S. was fighting in Vietnam never subsided. As a result, he has spent many years reading about Vietnam. His research has made him realize that there are no simple answers to the questions about U.S. involvement in Vietnam.